Dorothea Dix

Advocate for Mental Health Care

Silver Creek High School
3434 Silver Creek Rd
San Jose, CA 95121

DATE DUE

DEMCO, INC. 38-2931

OXFORD
PORTRAITS

Dorothea Dix

Advocate for Mental Health Care

Margaret Muckenhoupt

OXFORD
UNIVERSITY PRESS

To my husband, Scott, and to Ken Robey, the best boss I ever had.

OXFORD
UNIVERSITY PRESS

Oxford New York
Auckland Bangkok Buenos Aires Cape Town Chennai
Dar es Salaam Delhi Florence Hong Kong Istanbul Karachi Kolkata
Kuala Lumpur Madrid Melbourne Mexico City Mumbai Nairobi
São Paulo Shanghai Singapore Taipei Tokyo Toronto

Published by Oxford University Press, Inc.
198 Madison Avenue, New York, New York 10016
www.oup.com

Layout & Design: Greg Wozney

Library of Congress Cataloging-in-Publication Data
Muckenhoupt, Margaret.
Dorothea Dix : champion for the mentally ill / Margaret Muckenhoupt.
p. cm. — (Oxford portraits)
Includes bibliographical references and index.
ISBN 0-19-512921-0 (alk. paper)
1. Dix, Dorothea Lynde, 1802-1887–Juvenile literature. 2. Women social
reformers—United States—Biography—Juvenile literature. 3. Mentally ill—
Care—United States—History–Juvenile literature. [1. Dix, Dorothea Lynde,
1802-1887. 2. Reformers. 3. Mentally ill—Care—History. 4. Women—
Biography.] I. Title. II. Series.

HV28.D6 M83 2003
362.2'1'092--dc22

2003017874

9 8 7 6 5 4 3 2 1

Printed in the United States of America on acid-free paper

Cover: Portrait of Dorothea Dix by Samuel Bell Waugh, 1868
Frontis: Dorothea Dix, photographed in 1850

CONTENTS

Dorothea Dix had this portrait painted when she was 20 years old. Her warm voice and chestnut-colored hair impressed all who met her.

A GIRL BEGINS HER LONELY JOURNEY

It is strange that nobody noticed the girl traveling by herself. In 1814, the road from Worcester to Boston, Massachusetts, passed through villages with blacksmiths, lawyers, and doctors. There were inns for travelers along the way. Plenty of merchandise was carried in and out of New England's largest cities—wagons full of fish bound inland and flour riding out to the seaports. Still, no one stopped the girl, or asked where she was going, or helped her. Twelve-year-old Dorothea Dix made her first long journey alone.

In her later years, Dix's solitary travels were her life. She had no home, no fixed address at all. She made her reputation by constantly moving—and she kept changing places at least monthly until she went to her deathbed in New Jersey. Crisscrossing the United States, she single-handedly created most of the 19th-century public institutions east of the Mississippi River that served people with mental illness. She insisted that the government had an obligation to aid its most helpless citizens and that everyone—including prisoners, the poor, and people with mental illness—had a right to be treated with dignity. She was unyielding and effective, a symbol of women's good works.

At the same time, Dorothea Dix's life was a tale of arrogance and grief. Born at a time when New England was rapidly developing from a patchwork of farms to a network of cities, Dix was always slightly out-of-step and behind the times. She did not even begin her most important social reform work until she was 39 years old. Her fierce independence allowed her to act boldly and travel all over the United States and Europe at a time when most women quietly kept to their homes, but it also kept her from listening to valuable advice. Her life's greatest work—founding dozens of public hospitals for people with mental illnesses—was an enormous, selfless gift to her country. But in the end, Dix inadvertently created almost as much suffering for those patients as she relieved.

Dorothea Dix's family history was complicated by money, ambition, and battles over religion. Her grandfather, Elijah Dix, was a proud, bad-tempered man. Born in 1747, he built a successful medical practice in Worcester, a city 40 miles west of Boston. Aggressive and public-spirited, he organized dozens of plans for improving his town, from planting shade trees and founding a fire company to building the Worcester and Boston Turnpike.

Elijah Dix was too ambitious to limit himself to curing Worcester's ills. After the Revolutionary War, he sailed to Europe to visit a business partner who had supported the British and then escaped to England. Dix returned with medical supplies and European contacts for trade. He became rich by importing medicines and scientific instruments, and by 1795, Elijah Dix had enough money to build a mansion in Boston for his wife, Dorothy, and his three children.

The family was not quite in the social or financial position to live on Beacon Hill, Boston's most exclusive neighborhood. Instead, they settled on a street where several wealthy rum merchants lived. These men made their fortunes in the "triangular trade," which involved shipping rum to Africa, slaves from Africa to the West Indies, and

rum and slaves from the West Indies to Boston. Forty years later, Boston would become the hub of the movement to end slavery, but when Elijah Dix moved there, slavery was the basis for the fortunes of many prominent families.

The Dixes' brick mansion was called Orange Court, after its Orange Street address. Orange Court enclosed a garden—a sign of wealth in a crowded city—featuring the Dix Pear tree, bred by the Dixes. Newly rich merchants like Elijah Dix were thought to be in danger of loving money too much and developing hard hearts and narrow minds. The cure for the affliction of wealth was to raise pear trees. Rich men who raised fruit showed that they were rooted in their communities and had well-cultivated minds. By growing pears, wealthy traders could ensure that their souls would be secure, even as their fortunes grew.

The wharves were centers of trade in Boston. The owners of Yankee clipper ships, which docked in Boston, made fortunes.

Dorothea's father, Elijah, bred the Dix Pear. By creating the pear, the Dixes showed that they were benevolent citizens, interested in furthering the public good by creating nutritious fruit.

Unfortunately, the Dixes had more success raising their Dix Pear trees than their second son, Joseph. William Dix, their first son, became a prominent physician, and Polly, their daughter, married a promising young minister named Thaddeus Mason Harris; their three younger sons were respectable men as well. But their second son, Joseph, never really succeeded. Some relatives said that he was an alcoholic, or a gambler, or simply too sensitive to his father's violent temper.

Like a quarter of his classmates, Joseph dropped out of the Harvard College class of 1798; unlike the others, he did not use social connections to become a Boston businessman. Instead, in December 1800 he married a middle-class woman named Mary Biglow. There is not much that can be substantiated about Mary Biglow's family, and there is even confusion as to who she was—at least two women with identical or nearly identical names (Mary Biglow and Mary Bigelow) were living in the area at the time. By contrast, the Dixes were well-known because they were well-to-do. Joseph and Mary moved to one of his father's estates in Hampden, Maine, called Dixmont. His father did not give Joseph any of the land, but rather kept him as a manager—one of many signs that Elijah did not trust his second son.

On April 4, 1802, Mary Dix gave birth to Dorothea Lynde Dix, who was named after her rich grandmother. There is little record of her childhood, but her first years were marked by family disasters. Joseph's older brother, William, had died before Dorothea (nicknamed "Dolly") was born. Then, his three younger brothers lost huge amounts of money for the family business and died. President Thomas Jefferson, in an attempt to stop Britain and France from seizing American ships, declared an embargo on foreign goods—meaning that no merchandise could be shipped to the United States from Britain or France. The Dixes' import business was destroyed. In June 1809, Grandfather Elijah died. His will left Joseph with just a small anuity, but provided young Dorothea with an independent income until her marriage. Several of Elijah Dix's other heirs were also given pittances, and the family successfully fought the will. Joseph got one-tenth of the Dixmont land, but Dorothea got nothing.

Three years later, the War of 1812 broke out. The Dixes moved inland to avoid invasion by the British navy and settled in Barnard, Vermont, an isolated town in the hills of the Connecticut River valley.

Having dropped out of school, married below his social station, and moved to a tiny backwater town, Joseph Dix now rejected his family's religion. In Maine, he had attended the Congregationalist meetinghouse in Hampden, an indication that he was part of the same middle-of-the-road Protestant sect as most landowners and gentlemen. Once Joseph Dix arrived in Vermont, however, he swapped the Maine Dixmont land that he had inherited for books. Joseph had become a Methodist, and he opened a store selling sermons, pamphlets on doctrine, and stories from revival meetings. While many Congregationalists thought that Christians should slowly and gradually discipline themselves to save their souls, Methodists believed in dramatic, emotional religious conversions. Dorothea's later distaste for emotional outbursts may have been a reaction to her father's creed.

Ten-year-old Dorothea spent her time stitching together her father's reprints of pamphlets and books, a task she hated. She probably also spent time caring for her younger brothers; Charles was born in 1812, and Joseph in 1815. She was undoubtedly miserable. In her later life, she would not even admit to having parents. She claimed she had been an orphan, or she simply would not discuss the subject. Her life was probably not any worse than any other rural girl being raised by religious zealots. But she chose to run away, which indicates she was less content than most of her peers.

At age 12, she tried to escape. Dorothea traveled from Worcester, where her parents were visiting, to Boston by herself and appeared at the doorstep of her grandmother, Dorothy Lynde Dix. Madame Dix was not prepared to care for a young girl, and Dorothea was sent back to her parents.

In 1816, Madame Dix helped Dorothea leave home. She arranged for Dorothea to live in Worcester with Sarah Fiske, a niece who had married a doctor. If her experience was like that of other girls, the 14-year-old-Dorothea was treated as a young adult, not a child. She could stay as long as she earned her keep.

Most girls Dorothea's age helped with the "woman's work" at home, doing tasks such as weaving, knitting, baking bread, growing vegetables, brewing beer, washing, and making soap and candles. Some girls earned money by selling piecework—handmade hats, shoes, and clothing they crafted at home.

Dorothea's grandmother, Madame Dorothea Dix, at 76. A strong-willed woman, Madame Dix had many opinions about young Dorothea's life.

Dorothea, though, was staying with an upper-class doctor's family. Sarah Fiske certainly was not selling straw hats; her husband's money would have purchased the things that a farmer's wife made by hand. To prove herself useful, Dorothea Dix decided to become a teacher, and she opened a school in the house.

It was a logical choice. In 1816, there were very few ways for young middle-class women to earn money. Poor women could be servants and maids; almost the only jobs open to well-connected young girls like Dorothea Dix were doing piecework and teaching school. There was no state licensing board; the profession was open to anyone. Almost a quarter of Massachusetts women in Dix's generation taught school at some point. They were usually unmarried women between 17 and 30, but some teachers started when they were as young as 14, like Dorothea.

Still, it was an odd choice for Dix because she herself had never attended school; she was probably taught to read at home. Dix made up for her lack of knowledge through discipline. She lengthened her shirt sleeves and her skirts to look more grown-up, and she stood straight and tall. At five feet seven inches, she was an imposing figure before her class. She also spanked her students. One boy said, "It was her nature to use the whip, and use it she did." Only boys were whipped; girls were given more creative punishments. Dix forced one mischief-maker to walk through town wearing a sign declaring she was "A Very Bad Girl Indeed."

Dorothea Dix spent five years in Worcester with the Fiske family. In April 1821 her father died, leaving his wife and children no inheritance. Mary Dix moved to Fitzwilliam, New Hampshire, to live with relatives, most likely taking Dorothea's six-year-old brother, Joseph, with her. Nine-year-old Charles went to live with Dorothea. Madame Dix agreed to take in her now-adult granddaughter, and Dorothea and Charles moved to Boston to join their grandmother at Orange Court.

CONVERSATIONS

ON

COMMON THINGS;

OR,

GUIDE TO KNOWLEDGE.

WITH

QUESTIONS.

———◆———

FOR THE USE OF SCHOOLS AND FAMILIES.

Dorothea Lynde Dix

BY A TEACHER.

The taking a taste of every sort of knowledge is necessary to form the mind, and is the only way to give the understanding its due improvement to the full extent of its capacity.   LOCKE.

————————

THIRD EDITION,
REVISED, CORRECTED, AND STEREOTYPED.

BOSTON:
MUNROE AND FRANCIS,
128 Washington Street.

The title page from the third edition of Conversations on Common Things *includes a quote from British philosopher John Locke. Dix's books were best-sellers and gave her an independent income.*

2

"THE WORLD IS MY HOME"

During the American Revolution, Boston was a small town of 10,000 residents; by 1820, 43,000 people mobbed the streets. Energetic Bostonians were building an international city. They put up wharves and docks and even carted away the top 60 feet of Beacon Hill to fill in marshes. When Dorothea Dix arrived in 1821, Boston docks hosted ships brimming with British porcelain, Chinese tea, Caribbean rum, Hawaiian pineapples, and whale oil wrung from Arctic seas. Tradesmen shipped New England's timber and cod to the world and were setting up posts as far south as Savannah, Georgia, to sell New England's most reliable commodity: ice.

In the meantime, Dorothy Lynde Dix's fortune had shrunk to the point where she was living in a small cottage on her property and letting a tenant use the mansion as a boardinghouse. Dorothea and Charles joined the crowd of boarders. Dix later described the situation to her friend Anne Heath:

> [The] week before last one of our gentleman
> boarders departed on a journey: I did not know he

was out of town till the third day of his absence; another left the same week, was absent four days and was not missed till just before his return; a third left us for New York to be absent four weeks, and the first I knew of the matter was tonight at the tea-table; he went on Thursday!!!—Now what sort of existence is this think you?—Anne if you do not wish to live *with, by, and for yourself* (that is as regards the household) never go into a boarding house.

This arrangement was probably better for Dorothea than actually living with her grandmother, who constantly criticized Dorothea's needlework, religion, and the way she disciplined Charles. Fortunately, Dorothea did not have to rely on her relatives for inspiration. Dix was powerfully affected by the "Boston religion," the Unitarian movement, and faithfully attended two Sunday sermons at several churches each week.

Believers in a liberal Christian faith, the Unitarians took their name from their denial of the Trinity, the concept that God was divided into a Father, a Son (Jesus Christ), and a Holy Ghost, all equally divine. Instead, the Unitarians believed that God was only one spirit, and that Jesus Christ was a man—an important man, but only a man. This clash with traditional Christianity provoked furious battles for control of churches and many other Massachusetts institutions.

Most Unitarians were comfortable citizens who could afford pew rent, the charge for sitting in the church. Harriet Beecher Stowe, who would write the antislavery novel *Uncle Tom's Cabin* in later years, remembered that when her father arrived in Boston in 1825, "All the literary men of Massachusetts were Unitarian. All the trustees and professors of Harvard College were Unitarians. All the elite of wealth and fashion crowded Unitarian churches."

Perhaps the Unitarians' greatest virtue was self-restraint. They did not believe in sudden revolutions. The Unitarians believed that societal change, if it happened at all, was supposed to be gradual and slow, and supported by self-discipline. At Unitarian services, Dix was constantly exhorted to cultivate her moral character, restrain herself, and regulate her feelings. The Unitarians founded hospitals, public lecture series, and peace societies, and they gave money to other charitable causes—though these measures were meant to "improve" the poor by teaching them moral discipline, not just ease their suffering.

Dix thoroughly absorbed Unitarian principles and set to work. She asked to use the Orange Court barn as a schoolroom for "charitable and religious purposes." She wrote to her grandmother, "Why not when it can be done, without exposure or expense, let *me* rescue some of America's miserable children from vice and guilt, dependence on the Almshouse, and finally from what I fear will be their eternal misery." Dix gave her students a moral education, not a rigorous academic course. Her attitude reflected her own haphazard education. Instead of going to school, Dix had taught herself, and now, as an adult, she continued her studies by attending popular public lectures in Boston on a variety of topics—geology, fine arts, morality. She mastered enough astronomy and mineralogy to teach it to her students, and she learned other natural sciences in order to demonstrate the divine order that God had created in the world. Her favorite science was botany, the classification of plants. Dix adored flowers and loved sorting nature into groups and subgroups.

Her classes were successful, and in April 1824 she was offered a post teaching needlework at the new Boston Female Monitorial School run by William Bentley Fowle. An educational reformer, Fowle also introduced such classroom novelties as blackboards and spelling lessons to the United States. The monitorial method of instruction was a way of teaching many students at once using older children as instructors—the "monitors"—under a teacher's guidance. Using this method, Dix taught needlework to 70 girls at a time.

In May 1824 Dix reached out to an even larger audience with the publication of *Conversations on Common Things*. This book was a sort of mini-encyclopedia, in the form of a series of dialogues between a mother and her daughter. *Conversations* gave simple explanations of how useful things were made and used, along with lectures on the importance of hard work, self-control, and other favorite Dix topics. The subjects range from air to zinc, with topics such as coral, gunpowder, beeswax, and chocolate in between, all patiently explained by a loving mother.

Conversations was wildly successful, and it stayed in print for more than 40 years, bringing Dix a secure small income. It did not make Dix famous, however; the book's author was listed only as "A Teacher." Like many female authors of

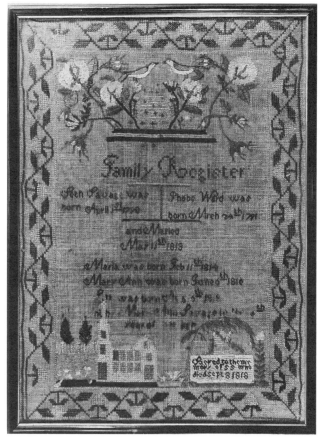

This sampler is typical of those stitched by New England women in the 1800s. Women kept their hands busy creating art from thread, stitching letters, flowers, and virtuous sayings.

the time, she felt that releasing books under her own name was unladylike, and published it anonymously.

Despite her success as a teacher and author, Dix felt unsettled. She feared that she might explode with emotion at any time. When the Marquis de Lafayette, the French hero of the American Revolution, visited Boston in 1824, Dix was presented to him at a posh Beacon Hill party. She kept her face in a sober grimace the whole time and wrote to her friend Anne Heath, "I long to see him; to be in the room with him and yet I hardly would trust myself . . . my feelings . . . would be under *no* control; tears and tears only would make my greetings—and speak my heart's language." Not all of Dix's passions were so selfless. In the letter about poet Laetitia Landon, Dix wrote, "I worship talents almost, I sinfully dare mourn that I possess them not." Dix craved Landon's ability and fame—cravings that were certainly not virtuous or charitable. She would never have taught the Monitorial School girls to have these sorts of ambitions. Reconciling her desires and her idea of moral behavior would prove very difficult for her in years to come.

Despite her serious intentions, Dix did not spend all her time trying to discipline herself. She found a soul mate in Anne Heath, whom she met in November 1822. Heath was five years older than Dix and lived in a farmhouse in a Boston suburb with her parents, four sisters, and two brothers. Dix yearned to have a large, loving family like Anne Heath's— so much that Dix forgot her own. In one letter, she wrote, "You dear Anne, in your admirable mother have one who may always put you right if you are tempted to go astray, but I wander alone, with none to guide me," even though her mother Mary Dix was quite alive in New Hampshire.

The two young women quickly developed a passionate friendship. Together, they shared their hopes and fears about their intellectual and spiritual improvement, discussing sermons or reading poetry together. They exchanged bouquets and gifts when they met, and between visits sent each other

MOTHER EXPLAINS A FACTORY

This excerpt from Converstaions on Common Things *(1824), Dorothea Dix's most successful book, explains Dix's theory of education. Studying any topic—including mechanical looms—is a worthy pursuit, and much more enjoyable than mere pastimes and play.*

Daughter: Why, mother, did you spend so much time in the factory the other day? I saw the spindles whirl till I was tired: do tell me why you looked so long at that great pile called machinery?

Mother: I will tell you, my dear; I wished to understand the principle upon which the spools and spindles were set in motion; the action of the looms; and closely to observe every part of what you thought so uninteresting.

Daughter: Of what use will it be to you, mother? You told me the other day I must have a reason for everything I do, and some useful end in view.

Mother: Suppose, Sarah, I should ever be asked if I had visited any of our manufactories, and answering in the affirmative, should be further questioned respecting the construction and management of them: should I not, think you, suffer some degree of mortification, if unable to give any explanation of their parts, and the principles upon which they are established; and would not my friends have reason to suppose me very stupid and ignorant: besides, does not the acquirement of any thing new to your understanding contribute to your lasting enjoyment in a higher degree, than mere superficial observation, or any pleasure you receive from the gratification of your appetite, or mere transient amusements?

flower petals and locks of hair, and drawerfuls of lengthy, heart-felt letters. Dix wrote of her beloved Anne, "My dreaming and my waking hours are alike given to the idea of mine friend," and also, "I so often dream of you that I shall come to identify facts with the images fertile fancy is ever producing, and possess a double store of pleasurable recollections having you for their object." Possessively, Dix often signed her letters with cautions like "Do not show or read any one this note." Heath returned Dix's affections, giving Dix the name Theadora in her letters, and crying miserably when she broke a trinket Dix had given her.

Anne Heath was not only a sister to Dix; she was a bridge to a new social world, which included young men. The Heaths entertained

Anne Heath stood straight and tall for this 1864 photograph. Dix's closest friend, Heath exchanged passionate letters with Dix while they were in their 20s.

young Unitarian ministers in their home, sincere, somber men who admired the tall and slender Dorothea, with her shining chestnut hair. But what visitors most noticed was her sweet voice. One observer noted that her voice was "so invariably potent in holding her listener at arm's length, it especially impressed me as a feature of her very marked individuality." For her part, Dix wrote excited letters to Heath about Ezra Stiles Gannett, an austere young Unitarian minister. Gannett was not one of Unitarian Boston's more gifted clergymen, but his calm and discipline appealed to Dix. Gannett never seemed to notice Dix though, or court her.

In the winter of 1824 Dix's relationship with Anne Heath began to break down. Anne's sister Mary died in

December at age 20. Anne was crushed, and Dix had no idea how to respond. Instead of comforting Heath, Dix pleaded for attention. At the funeral, Dix collapsed into a sobbing heap and wrote to Anne afterward that she could not control herself because she was so horribly, desperately lonely. She begged Anne to "Think oh! Think of the *treasure* you have still in possession. Anne, *I* have neither sister, nor *parent* . . . I am a being almost alone in this wide world." Afterward, the relationship was never as intense as before, though they remained friends.

Dix's persistence, even her insensitivity, may have caused suffering for Anne Heath, but it was the key to her future success. Dix would have to resist all common notions of how a woman was supposed to live to accomplish her goals. She needed her hard head and strong will; she also needed friends.

As Heath withdrew and found new friends, Dix became depressed and wrote to her, "I know not why I am so sad of late. I have daily and hourly cause of gratitude for numberless mercies, yet I feel there is a void that is most dreary." Dix decided to close her school at Orange Court and teach only at the Female Monitorial School.

Dix's grandmother also felt that something was missing from her granddaughter's life: The 23-year-old Dix did not seem to have any marriage prospects. Her grandmother coerced Dorothea into spending the winter of 1825–26 with relatives in Worcester and Milton, Massachusetts, in the hopes that they would prove better matchmakers than the Heaths.

Dorothea found quiet ways to resist her grandmother's schemes. In December 1825, she wrote from Milton, "*Company* I refuse *altogether* (balls and parties I mean) . . . I feel no desire to add to my frailties that of wasting time." When she reached Worcester in February, Dix immediately became ill and spent the entire month in bed. She recovered, however, a few days after she went home.

There, Dix decided that she had had enough of Orange Court as well. Her brother Charles had left school and was ready to become a sailor, and her grandmother was well cared for by her tenant. Dix had no reason to stay, and on May 1, 1826, she moved to a boardinghouse for young ladies in Boston. Dix had written Anne Heath in November, "*Home* did I say! The world is my home, I am a wanderer in the land where my fathers dwelt; a pilgrim where their hearth fires blazed; an isolated being, 'who walk among the crowd, not of it.'" Moving away from Orange Court, Dix was ready to face the world—alone.

This romanticized portrait surrounded by a garland of flowers, published in A Garland of Flora, *illustrates how sentimental Dix's writing had become. Few readers were interested in this book of gushing admiration for flowers.*

3

A TEACHER AND
AN AUTHOR

In May 1826, a Boston publisher asked Dorothea Dix to co-edit the first American magazine for children along with Lydia Maria Francis (later Child), a successful novelist and teacher. That same week, William Ellery Channing, the pastor of the Federal Street Church, asked Dix to lead a Sunday school class. Dix's work was getting noticed.

Both offers were flattering. At 24, Lydia Maria Francis was a literary celebrity, having written two acclaimed novels and a book for children similar to *Conversations*. Channing was the leading Unitarian minister in Boston. Pale, thin, and standing only five feet tall, he mesmerized congregations with his saintly gaze and soulful voice.

Dix rejected both offers, claiming that she was busy at the Monitorial School and that her health was uncertain. Channing persisted in recruiting her. He had met Dix through a mutual acquaintance, and had attended Harvard with Dix's father, Joseph Dix. Channing may have wanted to help his ne'er-do-well classmate's daughter or simply been impressed with her teaching. Dix finally agreed to teach a Sunday school class at the Monitorial School. Still, she never went to Channing's private Friday night meetings with his Sunday school teachers. She said that she did not want to risk her delicate health by walking in the cool night air. In a June 1826 letter to Anne Heath, Dix claimed, "I must study *alone* as I am condemned to *do every* thing alone I believe, in this life." Dix was not condemned, except by herself: she chose to be isolated.

Having preserved her leisure time from being taken up by her friends and mentors, Dix had ample time to write. During the winter of 1826–27, she began *Evening Hours*, a book of discussions on the Bible. After the first few chapters were published as short books, Dix began to write stories for a new book series called *Original Moral Tales for Children*. Her stories were full of children who struggled to control themselves and parents who encouraged them to subdue their tempers, be obedient, and work hard. Reading their Bibles and learning to be quiet, Dix's heroes and heroines are utterly sincere and completely humorless. She intended her stories to be moral instruction for young people, not entertainment.

In this illustration from Original Moral Tales for Children, *children do their lessons before a stern schoolmaster. Dix's writing fit perfectly with these moralistic stories of misbehavior, punishment, and redemption.*

While she was busy writing, Dix's health was failing. A series of chronic lung infections in the winter of 1826–27 kept her from the Monitorial School, until she finally resigned. William Bentley Fowle observed that her replacement, a 17-year-old student monitor, "soon spread over the school an air of order and industry which it had never exhibited before." Clearly, Dix had not been able to keep control of her class for some time.

During her young adulthood, Dix was frequently ill. She probably did not volunteer to be sick, but she used her illnesses to her advantage. Her various maladies let her sidestep her grandmother's matchmaking and escape an unruly classroom. In later life, when she was enthusiastically working for the good of the mentally ill, Dix was rarely sick, and even boasted about overcoming disease by willpower.

In April 1827, however, Dix was so ill that she permitted only ministers—and Anne Heath—to visit her. She revived when she accepted an invitation from William Ellery Channing to join his family at their house near Newport, Rhode Island. She was to take care of Channing's children, nine-year-old Mary and seven-year-old Willy, in exchange for room and board. In June, she left for Oakland, the Channing estate.

Dix spent the summer by the ocean, strolling through Channing's orchards and fields and admiring the stars. She took Mary and Willy off on long walks to learn natural history by examining plants, insects, and rocks. She acted like a family friend, not a stern teacher with a fixed curriculum—but as usual, she insisted on good behavior. When she left Newport in October, Dix decided to preserve her health by spending the winter with Unitarians in the mild climate of Philadelphia. But there she became terribly homesick. Anne Heath wrote only irregularly, and instead of praising her thoughtfulness, Channing chided Dix for writing to him when she ought to be resting. To make matters worse, rainy winter weather kept Dix from attending church.

STUDENT LETTERS

Dix's Orange Court students wrote daily letters to her about their behavior and spiritual progress. Some of them were affectionate, others were apologetic, and some expressed awe at Dix's incredible energy.

"You know, dear Miss Dix, that I told you just now that I could not do my composition, and isn't it singular I just read in Martha's letter Borridill's quotation from Mr. Gannett's sermon, 'An iron *will* can accomplish *everything.*' Dear Miss Dix, I *will have* this 'iron will,' and I *will do* and *be* all that you expect from your child."

"Please write me a note, dear teacher. I send you the paper in hopes that you will: do, please! The *'casket'* is ready, please fill it with *'jewels'*. Your child, Molly."

"I thought I was doing very well until I read your letter, but when you said that you were 'rousing to greater energy,' all my self-satisfaction vanished. For if you are not satisfied in some measure with yourself, and are going to do more than you have done, I don't know what I shall do. You do not go to rest until midnight, and then you rise very early."

"You wished me to be very frank with you, and tell you my feelings. I feel the need of some one to whom I can pour forth my feelings, they have been pent up so long. You may, perhaps, laugh when I tell you I have a *disease,* not of body but of mind. This is *unhappiness.* Can you tell me of anything to cure it? If you can, I shall indeed be very glad. I am in constant fear of my lessons, I am so afraid I shall miss them. And I think that if I do, I shall lose my place in the school, and you will be displeased with me."

"AUNTY, SWEET, VERY DEAR, SWEET AUNTY,—You asked me just now who I was Writing to. I did not Ans' you on purpose. Aunty! Aunty!! do you think I shal! shall! get my Bible!!! I want to be a good girl so!!! Don't you want me to! I know you do, do, do! Aunty!!! Now, Aunty, I want to be good very much, and i'l tell you what, let's you and I never speak together, but write little notes all the time. Tomorrow morning I want to find a little note on my pillow, if *you! are not busy.* Goodbye, dear Aunty."

In her boredom and isolation, Dix began writing two books—*Meditations for Private Hours*, a series of inspirational readings for each day of the week, and *The Pearl*, a book of children's stories much like her *Original Moral Tales*. At the same time, she attempted to enter the world of adult literature with *A Garland of Flora,* a strange collection of descriptions of flowers, botanical information, and "a storehouse of poetical sentiment and image," as the preface promises. Published in May 1829, *Garland* was not terribly popular, and after it came out, Dix stopped writing altogether.

Today, this action would be hard to understand. Dix was living almost entirely off her book royalties, and she stood to make even more money from continuing to write her children's stories. But she was unhappy with the direction her writing had taken, and may have been unhappy with the direction writing was taking her. In the introduction to *Garland*, Dix laments "our own scribbling and 'degenerate days,' when there are more writers than readers, and more talkers than thinkers." Dix may have preferred to be a thinker and reader rather than the writer she had become.

Throughout her life, Dorothea Dix had a very strong conventional sense of her role. As a woman, she was supposed to be humble and hard working and to give selflessly to others. A woman's best place was in the home, tending to children and husband, cooking and cleaning, and healing the sick with gentle care. In 1828, though, Dix was unmarried, on the verge of becoming an "old maid," and making money from books. Other women writers of the time faced the same dilemma: How could they humbly tend to their homes, yet make money by selling their work to the public? Many women published their works under men's names or anonymously; others battled for a new definition of womanhood—one that included earning and keeping money under their own names (at the time, a married woman's money was legally owned by her husband). Dix avoided the issue by not writing any more books.

In the summer of 1829, Dix made two decisions: she would return to Boston and open another school and she would rent a house for herself and her brothers. By September, she had set up her own household, a declaration that she was not going to be keeping house for a husband. Dix was not going to have a conventional life.

Unlike their sister, Charles and Joseph were not terribly interested in school. Fourteen-year-old Joseph looked for a job, and seventeen-year-old Charles wanted to go to sea. Dix busied herself with preparations for her students, and easily found students to fill her classes. In her spare time, she sent seaweed samples she had collected along with letters to Benjamin Silliman, editor of the *American Journal of Science and Arts,* the most prestigious academic journal in the country. Dix also wrote an article on insect metamorphosis for the *Journal,* and she described a spider that the Channings had kept in a jar at Oakland in another article published in the *Journal* in January 1831. It was the last piece she published for eight years.

In August 1830, Dix accepted the Channings' invitation to join them on a winter trip to the Danish West Indies. She closed up her school and moved her brothers back to Orange Court, where her friends visited Charles and Joseph and showed them Dorothea's letters.

Landing on St. Croix in mid-December, the party quickly made its way into the countryside. Dix was aghast at the way that the colonists had destroyed the natural beauty of the island. She informed Torrey, a Boston friend and member of Channing's Federal Street Church, that instead of the enormous palm trees travelers found on "less *sacrificed*" islands, in St. Croix "now upon every hill, and down every valley, and far over all the level country, are spread the unbroken surface of Cane plantations."

Dix saw how sugarcane plantations degraded the environment; she did not perceive how they crushed human souls. The plantation where Dix and the Channings stayed housed 230 slaves. She wrote to friends in Boston about their dancing but never about the forced labor that dominated the slaves' lives. Dix told Torrey that the "managers, overseer, and too often the owners, are *very* corrupt," yet she believed that laws and the self-interest of the owners would keep the slaves from being abused. When discussing the efforts of Moravian missionaries to set up schools for slaves, Dix argued that it was a waste of time, because the slaves could not think for themselves. She declared that the slaves were "*not free agents,*" and went on to say, "I would by no means teach them the distinctions of right and wrong. I would not enlighten them, to ensure *a tenfold* wretchedness

This slave working on a Caribbean sugar plantation faced hours of back-breaking work each day. Conditions were harsh, and claimed the lives of most of the slaves.

here, and perhaps not make any progress in aiding them to be happier hereafter."

In part, Dix may have seen slavery as just one aspect of the Caribbean's "beautiful atmosphere of moral depravity," as she described it to Torrey. The island had few churches, many islanders drank alcohol heavily, and very few white residents ever bothered to do any work. All these failings horrified the self-controlled, self-righteous New Englander, who responded by trying to follow ever-stricter rules for her own conduct. Writing to Torrey, she declared that New Englanders must seek "more earnest self-discipline when we feel our firmer principles rising in indignation at transgressions which perhaps only a more correct early education has taught us to view with proper disgust and horror." In another letter, she told Torrey that when she saw near-naked children and adults, "one's delicacy is at first shocked by such novel exhibitions," but "feelings accommodate themselves to circumstances." Dix was determined to control herself at all costs—and at a high cost to her moral integrity.

Dix's bigotry at St. Croix did not keep her from being exquisitely sensitive to human misery in her later life. It is also likely that Dix did not know that the slave population of St. Croix had been declining for decades, due to overwork, poor nutrition, and disease. Yet William Ellery Channing later wrote of St. Croix, "Here was a volume on slavery opened always before my eyes, and how could I help learning some of its lessons?" Somehow, Dix could not see the same page.

At the same time, though, Boston abolitionists—activists who worked to end slavery—were dismayed at how slowly Channing came to denounce slavery. He thought that the abolitionists were extremists, and disagreed with their demonization of Southern planters—a view that Dix shared. Although Channing deplored slavery, he preached that slaves should be freed gradually, and that slave owners

William Ellery Channing was known for his pale face and "saintly gaze." Dix's friend and mentor, he encouraged her religious devotion.

should be paid for their losses. When Channing finally did publish a book denouncing slavery in 1835, it alienated many of his Federal Street parishioners who had gotten rich trading Southern cotton. Many Bostonians shared Dix's and Channing's sympathy for the South and suspicion of the abolitionists.

When she was not writing on St. Croix, Dix spent some time examining her collections of tropical seaweeds, but she did little else. She refused to go outside in the heat. "I pant under the *weight* of muslins and Cambrics," she wrote to Torrey.

In May 1831, Dix returned with the Channings to the "invigorating air of New England." Almost immediately, she confronted a family crisis; her grandmother's longtime tenant announced that she would be leaving. Feeling responsible for her grandmother, Dix decided to move back to Orange Court and run a school for teenage girls on the grounds.

Dix opened her school at a promising time. Americans were beginning to take women's education seriously. In a speech to the American Institute of Instruction in August 1831, George B. Emerson, headmaster of Boston's foremost school for young ladies, argued that girls should learn algebra and geometry, Latin, physical sciences, and essay writing, in contrast to a more typical curriculum of French, music, painting, and dancing. As mothers and teachers, educated women would "give a permanent impulse to the onward movement of the race," Emerson said.

Dix was not as progressive as Emerson, however. Her school did not offer either algebra or more than elementary Latin, but she did teach a great deal of botany and natural history. She drilled students in grammar and had them write letters instead of essays. A French tutor worked at the school, but students had to pay extra fees for tutors in music, drawing, and dancing. Dix taught all the other courses herself. One student described the conditions: "The arrangements of the school were very primitive—no desks for the girls, only a long table through the middle of the room, at which we sat for meals, and at which it was very inconvenient to write." Students helped with chores because Dix never hired any caretakers apart from one young woman apprentice from the Boston poorhouse.

Dix's school was never advertised or named. Her pupils were from well-to-do families, generally referrals from friends, parishioners from Channing's church, or former students from the Monitorial School. These parents were not buying first-rate intellectual educations for their children; they were entrusting their daughters to the moral and spiritual care of Miss Dix. Each day, she held morning and evening religious services, and she taught a religion class as well. Boarding students went through a Saturday evening "private interview," a sort of confession, and went to Sunday services at the Federal Street Church. Dix also set up a spiritual post office—a large conch shell from St. Croix, where students would drop daily letters about their progress and their well-examined lives.

For this uplifting experience, Dix charged four times the tuition of the Monitorial School. Most female schoolteachers were earning $200 to $250 per year, or about $3,000 to $4,000 in today's dollars; at her peak enrollment of 30 students, Dix would have taken in ten times as much before expenses.

Many students adored Dix, calling her "Aunty," but other pupils resented her strictness. Writing to one backslider,

"I Am Now Obliged to Refuse You the Desired Gratification"

"The Prize" was one of Dorothea Dix's typical stories for children—a tale of a misbehaving, willful girl and her patient father. In the excerpt below, Anna makes the mistake of losing her temper.

Anna, at length tired of waiting for an answer, exclaimed, in an exceedingly impatient tone, "Do tell me, father, may I go walk with you?"

"Anna, that impatient and violent temper of yours will make you miserable," said Mr. Fitzgerald, looking on his child in sorrow; "it is for *this very* fault of yours, which you are perfectly so sensible you possess, that I am now obliged to refuse you the desired gratification. I was not at home yesterday, it is true, but—"

Anna interrupted her father by a passionate burst of tears; she was not willing to hear any thing her father continued to say—and though she did not make the least attempt to deny her fault, yet she increased it tenfold, and to all her father's endeavors to pacify and reason with her, she returned only passionate exclamations, and violent and renewed bursts of tears! Her father then whistled to Frisk, and walked calmly out of the house, leaving his rebellious little girl to recover herself at her leisure.

Dix insisted, "I have but one object in teaching; it is to aid the *spirit upward. Whatever* tends to the accomplishment of this end, I adopt, however *unpopular* it may be for the *time being.*" This harsh discipline took its toll over time. By January 1835, only 9 out of 30 pupils were left.

While Dix's students were disappearing, her family was vanishing as well. Charles Dix left with a merchant ship to Europe, and Joseph sailed to Asia, leaving Dix alone with her sickly 90-year-old grandmother.

Under the stress of caring for her disintegrating school and frail grandmother, Dix broke down in March 1836. Writing to George B. Emerson, Dix announced that she was deathly ill, though she never said exactly what was wrong, and that she planned to leave for Europe as soon as she could. Traveling abroad was supposed to provide Dix with a calmer climate than Boston's winter and release her from the stress of work. Emerson found new schools for Dix's few remaining students and concluded, "Miss Dix was a thorough, successful Teacher, and got rich, but she did not succeed in making her scholars *love her.*"

On April 16, Dix set off for Liverpool, England, with the family of a former student, Joaquina Fesser. Edward Fesser, Joaquina's father, took away Dix's pens and paper to keep her from exhausting herself, but she managed to nurse a sick young woman who died shortly after the ship reached Liverpool. Then, Dix herself collapsed. The Fessers cared for her in their Liverpool hotel until Edward's business forced them to leave for London. They left her with the wealthy Rathbone family at their Greenbank estate, three miles from Liverpool, where Dix would stay for more than a year.

The Unitarian Rathbones were happy to host Dix, especially when they learned that she knew William Ellery Channing, who had stayed at their estate. They were also familiar with Americans: The family's trading business had helped arrange the first shipment of American cotton to

England. By the time Dix got there, William Rathbone was so rich that he spent most of his time on politics.

The Rathbones were not only wealthy but also patient. After a few days with them, Dix wrote to her grandmother, "My restoration will undoubtedly be very gradual," and it was. During her yearlong stay, Dix only left Liverpool for a brief trip to England's Lake District with her doctor and his family. Despite Liverpool's damp, cold air and coal smoke, at Greenbank Dix was treated with an excellent medicine: love. The many Rathbones visited her throughout the day, leaving her in "a uniform state of cheerfulness," as she wrote to her grandmother.

Dix's friends were confused by her illness, guessing that it was caused by her long journey or overwork. William Ellery Channing suspected that she had made herself sick, and wrote to Dix, "Did you never hear the comparison of certain invalids to a spinning top, which is kept up by perpetual whirling? It was very natural that you should fall, when exciting motion ceased." Dix never said precisely what her illness was—just that "*rest* seems to be my necessity— long *positive inactivity*," as she wrote to Anne Heath.

In April 1837, Dix, still smarting from her friend's doubts, had a Unitarian Minister named John Hamilton Thom send a letter about her health to William Ellery Channing. Thom had corresponded with Channing briefly a few years before, and was engaged to marry one of the Rathbone daughters. Thom reported that Dix's doctor believed she would recover, but "the active part of her life must be considered over." Thom also reported on Dix's mental state, saying that "it is impossible to see any thing of so devotional a spirit, & so pure a conscientiousness without a strengthened confidence in the power & beauty of those principles of mind." He continued in a less complimentary vein,

I should fear that even in her most active benevolence there had been a want of the self forgetfulness which is the healthiest condition of the mind. I do not mean this in a selfish sense, far from it—but that her plans & hopes for others were too much regarded as proceeding from herself—& never sufficiently separated from the thought of her own individuality.

Dix suffered a relapse a few days after Thom wrote his letter, and she wrote to her friend Mary Torrey that "now it is less easy to maintain a perfectly regulated and tranquil mind than through the winter."

Dix was weary of being sick. She was still resisting her grandmother's orders to return home, though. Her grandmother wrote to Dix to say that she had been a heavy burden for the Rathbones and did not seem to be getting any healthier. On May 16, Dix wrote back, rejecting a cross-Atlantic journey as "absolutely out of the question as impracticable," and announced that she would stay abroad. Shortly afterward, Dix learned that her grandmother had died. She changed her mind and decided to return to the United States.

On August 24, after imploring the Rathbones to write to her, Dix left Liverpool for Rhode Island, to stay with the Channings.

BEGINNING THE
GREAT WORK

Dorothea Dix lingered at the Channings' estate in Rhode Island before she finally returned to Orange Court in October 1837. Once there, she found that although her grandmother's will had specified that she and her brothers would divide the house with her uncle Thaddeus Mason Harris, the executor of the will had sold the house to her uncle. Fortunately, she could afford to live on her own. Dix still had savings from her writing and teaching, and she had inherited one-sixth of her grandmother's estate—about $4,000, or almost $60,000 in today's dollars. Dix was also frugal and had plain tastes. She had started wearing dark dresses with a small white ruffle at the neck as the only decoration, and styled her hair in a simple coil at the back of her head.

Still, Dix did not *want* to live by herself. Compared to Greenbank, Boston was a lonely place. At age 35, Dix had no permanent home. She traveled and stayed with friends until December 1839, when she decided to rejoin the Channings. She moved into the house of William Ellery Channing's sister-in-law Sarah Gibbs, at the summit of respectable Beacon Hill, and Channing and his family soon

Public "asylums" were hazardous places in Dix's time. In this sensationalized woodcut, inmates are kept behind bars and refused help even as a fire rages through their cell.

moved into a townhouse on the Gibbs property. Dix was finally "*at home* and *at ease,*" as she told Anne Heath, and she spent her evenings reading to the minister.

Life continued comfortably for Dix until a Harvard Divinity School student asked her to take over his Sunday school class at the Middlesex County House of Correction in East Cambridge. Dix went there on March 28, 1841. At the end of her class, Dix walked across the yard to a small jail that held public drunks, poor men paying their debts by making shoes, and people who were mentally ill. According to state law, Middlesex County prisons had to have "a suitable and convenient apartment or receptacle for idiots and lunatic or insane persons, not furiously mad." Dix saw several "insane persons" crowded in rooms without a fire to warm them in the cold, damp New England spring. When she asked the warden to build a fire, he said that the flames would be dangerous and that it was not really necessary.

What happened next changed Dix's life. She immediately went next door to the county courthouse and complained about the cold cells. The court granted her wish, and the cells were heated. Dix had gone to the government to demand an end to cruelty, and she had stopped the abuse—by herself.

The victory energized Dix. Not only did she keep teaching at the prison school, but she bought religious books for her class, arranged for ministers to preach there, and started touring every public institution she could find. She soon confronted broader social dilemmas. In July she wrote to wealthy Federal Street Church member Nathan Appleton for funds to create a permanent library of religious and moral books at the East Cambridge prison. Appleton had made a great deal of money by constructing and operating the textile mills in Lowell, Massachusettes, where thousands of young women and men worked at gigantic mechanized looms, making cloth. Dix noted in her letter that most of the female prisoners in Cambridge had worked in the mills, as had many of the male prisoners, implying that the mill corrupted workers. Appleton pooh-poohed her attack, claiming that the mill business was wholesome employment for young women. In response, Dix sent back all of Appleton's donated books, and began researching how industrial labor harmed women.

Dix was reacting to a fundamental change in women's lives. In the new, strange order, girls left their families not for apprenticeships or relatives' homes, but to become a nameless, replaceable part of a giant industrial machine. They arrived in their teens, and generally left by the time they were 25 to marry and start families. Hundreds of unsupervised young women were free to do whatever they pleased with what little time they had left after the mill shift each day and on Sundays. In some ways, they were neglected and dehumanized; in others, they were more free than they

Workers, from children to old women, walk to their factory jobs. Dix feared that the new mills would have a negative effect on young women as they left their homes and families for a regimented life in unfamiliar company.

were on their families' farms, where they worked without pay. Like many other socially conservative New Englanders, Dix felt that mill work was harmful to young women.

At the same time, Dix was beginning to think of teaching again. On March 11, 1841, she visited the Massachusetts State Normal School, the first state school for teachers, to consider working there. Founded by Horace Mann, the Massachusetts secretary of education, the school was supposed to ensure that teachers would have standard training and knowledge—the sort of requirements that would have barred Dix from the field. Cyrus Peirce, the school's principal, hoped Dix would serve as a school matron, "as the older friend and adviser to the young ladies," as Dix and her conch shell had done at the old Orange Court school.

In August, Peirce and Mann formally asked Dix to be the matron at the Normal School. Reluctant to leave the Channings, Dix offered to go to the school three times a week and hire staff to run the boardinghouse. In exchange, she asked for complete control over the students' lives. She would keep the Normal School women from walking with gentlemen, or even from seeing them face to face; they would communicate only by letter, and the girls would be prohibited from even going to the post office to pick up the letters! Peirce, disturbed by Dix's plans, wrote to Mann, "The good lady must not expect to make these normalers *young ladies* in the sense in which her own scholars were. They are designed for a somewhat different sphere & must see & encounter more of the roughness of Life."

Peirce and Mann decided to withdraw their offer, and dispatched Samuel Gridley Howe, the versatile director of the Perkins Institute for the Blind, to let her know. Howe wrote to Dix in September 1841 and said that her proposal was "too generous & self-sacrificing on your part to be accepted," and that he, Peirce, and Mann "thought we knew so much better than you could what a great weight of care and anxiety it would devolve upon you—& therefore

Horace Mann, often called the father of American public education, founded the Massachusetts Normal School. Dix applied for a position at the school, which educated public school teachers.

decided for you." Dix was still free to accept the position, they decided, but only if she agreed to furnish the board-inghouse. Dix wisely declined the insulting offer.

Howe and Dix kept in touch afterward, talking about the care of the "insane," one of his pet interests. Exhausted from teaching at the prison and working to improve conditions there, Dix spent the winter of 1841 at home. Howe spent the season in Kentucky, lobbying for the construction of a state institute for the blind and talking with a young physician named Edward Jarvis.

Jarvis believed in the "moral treatment" of mental illness. In his pamphlet titled *Insanity and Insane Asylums*, he described the difference between "heroic treatment" of

45

mental illness, meant to fatigue and exhaust patients, and "moral treatment," meant to help patients develop self-control. Heroic treatment often involved powerful, dangerous drugs, such as ipecac (to induce vomiting), strong laxatives, or narcotics such as opium or morphine. Moral treatment, on the other hand, involved keeping patients in asylums, where the daily routine, hobbies, and jobs available would help them become calm and where they could listen to the kindly counsel of the asylum staff. This treatment stressed the need for a controlled environment, hard work, and discipline. Dix may not have read Jarvis's pamphlet, but the ideas in it would probably have appealed to her; she had put many of them into practice in her Orange Court school.

By June 1842, Dix had begun to work with Howe to reform treatment of the mentally ill in Massachusetts. Throughout the 1830s, towns in that state had rapidly constructed almshouses to house citizens with no relatives or neighbors who could care for them. The almshouses took in people with chronic physical or mental illnesses, the disabled, orphans, the elderly, and the unemployed. Demanding obedience, discipline, and hard work, the almshouses assumed the role families and churches had filled earlier. In an age when New Englanders were turning from farms to factories for their income, and women were working in schools and textile mills instead of staying home, the traditional social safety nets were falling apart. Towns tried to reweave them with new institutions.

Dix began systematically counting the residents in almshouses and jails and taking notes on their physical and mental state. Never one to neglect the spirit, Dix also looked at how often ministers visited and whether there were Sunday school classes. She handed her observations over to Howe, and planned to start examing the problems of the girls at the Lowell mills.

On September 8, Howe published an exposé in the Boston *Daily Advertiser* revealing East Cambridge's treat-

MORAL TREATMENT

Dorothea Dix promoted the "moral treatment" of people with mental illness, instead of the "heroic treatments" of the time, which usually involved powerful drugs and physical pain. Dr. Edward Jarvis, one of the leading proponents of moral treatment, outlined his approach in his Autobiography, *writing about himself in the third person. Jarvis worked with Samuel Gridley Howe, Dix's friend and supporter, to improve conditions in the Middlesex County House of Correction, where Dix fought to have stoves lit to warm people with mental illness.*

K nowing that so much depends on the influences which surround the patients, Dr. J. regulated every thing in respect to its effect on them—their food, their exercise, the places and the persons they visited or who visited them, the conversation at table or elsewhere. As some were disturbed by a certain diet, this was denied, and adapted to each one according to his especial peculiarity. As they are disturbed by certain persons, or ideas, or suggestions, these were arranged with the same view. Some of Dr. Jarvis's friends—his best— even caused painful associations to some of the patients, and such were requested not to visit them, or as long as he remained susceptible of excitement by their presence. . . .

As the cautious physician regulates and controls, so far as he can, all the food that reaches or affects the digestive organs of his dyspeptic patients, so the private manager of mental disorders must regulate all the language, books, conversation, scenes, suggestions, everything that can affect the cerebral organs. By this means he keeps the mind in a healthy action, withdraws it from unhealthy actions, and allows it to recover its healthy tone.

ment of the insane as "disgraceful in the highest degree to a Christian community." The prison physician objected and published a public letter in the *Advertiser* denying Howe's charges. Howe asked Dix to help support his claims. As Dix was pondering whether to continue working with Howe, William Ellery Channing died of typhoid fever in Vermont. Dix's surrogate father was dead, and her household was about to vanish as Sarah Gibbs moved in with Channing's wife, Ruth. Once again, Dix had no home.

On the day that Channing died, Dix wrote an article supporting Howe that was published the next day in

Nineteenth-century "asylums" often just housed people with mental illnesses, and it was not unusual to find inmates crowded together with no care or treatment offered.

Boston's *Evening Mercantile Journal.* She stated that the conditions in East Cambridge, though terrible, were far better than in other Massachusetts prisons and that she would soon reveal the whole awful situation to the world. Then Dix got to work. The victims chained in jails needed her; the Lowell mill girls would have to help themselves.

By December, she had traveled from the Cape Cod seashore to the Berkshire Mountains and back, visiting 35 towns in one week. "If I fail in this work," she wrote to Anne Heath, "it shall be through no negligence of mine." In previous years, Dix would have exhausted herself and fallen into her sickbed with such a schedule. Now, though, she did not have that alternative: who would take care of her? The Rathbones were in England. The Channings had their own sorrows. Dix had her work.

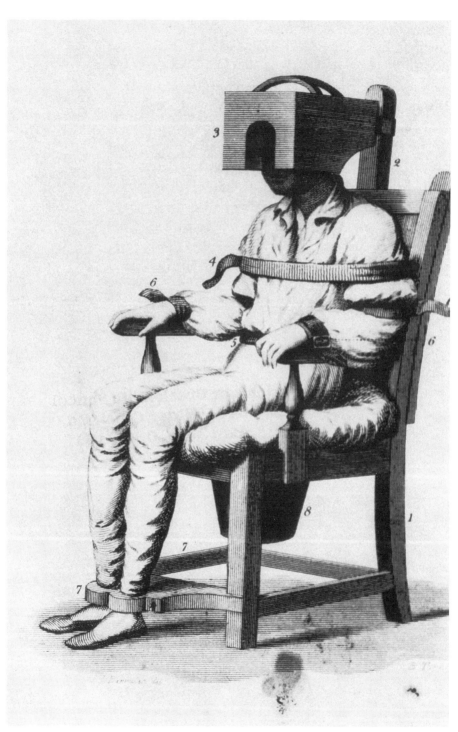

This "tranquilizing chair" was meant to soothe patients by immobilizing them. Many 19th-century treatments for mental illness were cruel and ineffective and were intended to restrain patients, not cure them.

"I Shall Be Obliged to Speak with Great Plainness"

In the 19th century, words like *insane* and *lunatic* referred to a broad class of people whose thoughts and behavior were not tolerated by their families and communities. Dorothea Dix herself referred to the people she helped as "insane." Today, those words and others such as *madman* are insults and trivialize the struggles of people with mental illness. Modern medicine views mental illnesses as conditions that can be treated with a combination of psychotherapy and drugs—just like heart disease or other diseases that attack the body.

While Dix was traveling around Massachusetts and surveying facilities, Samuel Gridley Howe was elected to the Massachusetts House of Representatives. In December he asked Dix to write a report for the state legislature, called a "memorial," about "the result of your painful & toilsome tour." Dix wrote the memorial and had Howe present it to the legislature on January 19, 1843.

Dix's *Memorial to the Legislature of Massachusetts* is a masterpiece of horror. The author of *Original Moral Tales for Children* now described "the *present* state of Insane Persons confined within this Commonwealth, in *cages, closets, cellars, stalls, pens! Chained, naked, beaten with rods,* and *lashed* into obedience!" Although Dix reported that the condition of most inmates "could not and need not be improved," she depicted a large minority "whose lives are the saddest picture of human suffering and degradation." Their keepers were more concerned with cutting expenses than with their prisoners' comfort. Men and women were chained to walls, and some lost their feet to frostbite when their keepers forgot to build fires in the winter. In one case, a guard left his charge in a shack next to "'the dead room,' affording in lieu of companionships with the living, a contemplation of corpses!"

There are no summaries or statistics in the *Memorial*; the closest Dix came to stating a number was to say that she had seen "hundreds of insane persons in every variety of circumstance and condition," during her travels. Instead, Dix declared, *"I tell what I have seen."*

A woman with mental illness is beaten and her head is dunked into cold water. These "cures" did not help anyone; the victims may have become more submissive, but torture was never an effective medical treatment.

Popular Mode of Curing Insanity!
Lizzie Bonner punishing Miss Hodson, on suspicion of taking her key.   See page 336.

text continues on page 55

"I Tell What I Have Seen!"

Below is an excerpt from Dix's Memorial to the Legislature of Massachusetts, *presented on January 19, 1843. It addressed the care of patients with mental illness and was Dix's first foray into politics; popular reaction to the report inspired Massachusetts legislators to enlarge the state psychiatric hospital by 60 percent.*

I shall be obliged to speak with great plainness, and to reveal many things revolting to the taste, and from which my woman's nature shrinks with peculiar sensitiveness. But truth is the highest consideration. *I tell what I have seen*—painful and shocking as the details often are—that from them you may feel more deeply the imperative obligation which lies upon you to prevent the possibility of a repetition or continuance of such outrages upon humanity. . . . I have seen many who part of the year, are chained or caged. The use of cages all but universal; hardly a town but can refer to some not distant period of using them. . . . I will tell you, my dear; I wished to understand the principle upon which the spools and spindles were set in motion; the action of the looms; and closely to observe every part of what you thought so uninteresting.

[In the town of Danvers] . . . Found the mistress, and was conducted to the place, which was called "*the home*" of the *forlorn* maniac, a young woman, exhibiting a condition of neglect and misery blotting out the faintest idea of comfort, and outraging every sentiment of decency . . . there she stood with naked arms and disheveled hair; the unwashed frame invested with fragments of unclean garments, the air so extremely offensive, though ventilation was afforded on all sides save one, that it was not possible to remain beyond a few moments without retreating for recovery to the outward air. Irritation of body, produced by utter filth and exposure, incited her to the horrid process of tearing off her skin by inches; her face, neck, and person, were thus disfigured to hideousness; she held up a fragment just rent off; to my exclamation of horror, the mistress replied, "oh, we can't help it; half the skin is off sometimes; we can do nothing with her; and it makes no difference what she eats, for she consumes her own filth as readily as the food which is brought her."

Men of Massachusetts, I beg, I implore, I demand pity and protection for these of my suffering, outraged sex. Fathers, husbands, brothers, I would supplicate you for this boon; but what do I say? I dishonor you, divest you at once of Christianity and humanity, does this appeal imply distrust. If it comes burdened with a doubt of your righteousness in this legislation, then blot it out; while I declare confidence in your honor, not less than your humanity. Here you will put away the cold, calculating spirit of selfishness and self-seeking; lay off the armor of local strife and political opposition; here and now, for once, forgetful of the earthly and perishable, come up to these halls and consecrate them with one heart and one mind to works of righteousness and just judgment.

Become the benefactors of your race, the just guardians of the solemn rights you hold in trust. Raise up the fallen, succor the desolate, restore the outcast, defend the helpless, and for your eternal and great reward receive the benediction, Well done, good and faithful servants, become rulers over many things!

This sentence was the heart of Dix's power. Presenting the *Memorial* to the state legislature put Dix in a tricky position. She needed to convey a strong political message without seeming so forward and unwomanly that the legislators would ignore her. Shrewdly, she used her femininity to justify her work. She said that she had a woman's sympathy with the victims of cruelty; seeing the horrors she described had forced her into unnatural, unfeminine behavior. Working with the legislature, she claimed, compelled her to give up "my habitual views of what is womanly and becoming." Because she could not run for office or make money from her surveys, Dix was seen as incorruptable, even when she was lobbying legislators. She could not gain power or money from her work, so people believed that her sole motivation was her own virtue, the goodness of her heart, and her sympathy with the victims of torture and injustice. Even as she moved in powerful political circles, Dix could appear as a perfect model of womanhood—a lady who was unconcerned with wealth and worldly accomplishment, and who was concerned only with being good.

Dix did not care about how a person came to be chained in a cell. The government's obligation was the same whether citizens drank themselves into a stupor or collapsed while working in the mills. The "insane" had to be removed from the prisons and almshouses and given a peaceful environment where they would be respected and kept safe. Dix's suggestion for government action in the *Memorial* was to set up a new asylum for people with incurable mental illness, so that all mentally ill inmates could be removed from prisons. Then, the inmates could work on their true task: regaining self-control and connection to God.

Her views strongly reflected her Unitarian faith, especially her faith in the powers of personal discipline. Dix's goal for the mentally ill was the right relations with God, not perfect mental health. To Dix, insanity was not degrading or evil. She wrote in the *Memorial* that only "the mortal part" disappeared "when the temple of reason falls in ruins." The "insane" still had feelings, and responded to kindness. They suffered because their emotions were uncontrolled. "It may be supposed that paroxysms of frenzy are often exhibited, and that the tranquil state is rare in comparison with that which incites to violence." Their self-mutilation, cries, threats, and screams kept them apart from God, and thoughtless, cruel jailers provoked "the passions which an iron rule might be expected to stimulate and sustain." Only when they became calm and disciplined, would the "insane" reach God. They would not necessarily be cured, but they would be at peace.

After Dix presented her work to the legislature, the *Memorial* was reprinted in pamphlets and excerpted in newspapers. It raised passionate emotions—and opposition. Some politicians fought Dix over the expense. Building a new state hospital the size of the current facility, located in Worcester, would cost $100,000 (almost $1.5 million today), or a quarter of the state's annual budget. Other officials complained that Dix had exaggerated. The town of Danvers charged that Dix had been in its almshouse for only five minutes. Shelburne officials claimed that Dix had created "bare-face falsehoods, false impressions, and false statements." Even sympathetic friends asked Dix how much of what she wrote was true.

Dix's supporters did not defend her work. Instead, they praised her feminine character. Throughout her life, Dix was treated not as a reformer but as a *woman* reformer. On February 6, 1843, the editor of the *Newburyport Herald* stated that Dix's work showed "that the heart of one woman is worth more than all the heads and hearts in the capitol." Referring to Dix's inability, as a woman, to run for political office, Boston's *Mercantile Journal* declared on February 21, "There appears to be no possible *motive* for this lady to misrepresent."

Samuel Gridley Howe chaired the Massachusetts state legislature's Committee on Public Charitable Institutions,

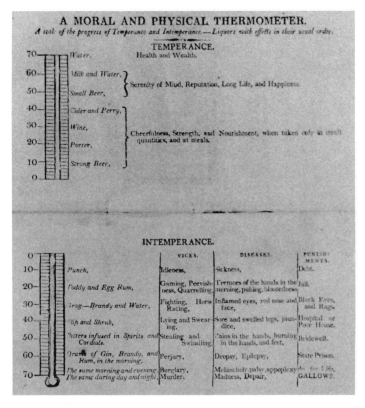

A MORAL AND PHYSICAL THERMOMETER.

A scale of the progress of Temperance and Intemperance.—Liquors with effects in their usual order.

TEMPERANCE.

70	Water,	Health and Wealth.
60	Milk and Water,	
50	Small Beer,	Serenity of Mind, Reputation, Long Life, and Happiness.
40	Cider and Perry,	
30	Wine,	
20	Porter,	Cheerfulness, Strength, and Nourishment, when taken only in small quantities, and at meals.
10	Strong Beer,	
0		

INTEMPERANCE.

		VICES.	DISEASES.	PUNISHMENTS.
0				
10	Punch,	Idleness,	Sickness,	Debt.
20	Toddy and Egg Rum,	Gaming, Peevishness, Quarrelling,	Tremors of the hands in the morning, puking, bloatedness	Jail.
30	Grog—Brandy and Water,	Fighting, Horse Racing,	Inflamed eyes, red nose and face,	Black Eyes, and Rags.
40	Flip and Shrub,	Lying and Swearing,	Sore and swelled legs, jaundice,	Hospital or Poor House.
50	Bitters infused in Spirits and Cordials,	Stealing and Swindling,	Pains in the hands, burning in the hands, and feet,	Bridewell.
60	Drams of Gin, Brandy, and Rum, in the morning,	Perjury,	Dropsy, Epilepsy,	State Prison.
70	The same morning and evening, The same during day and night,	Burglary, Murder,	Melancholy, palsy, appoplexy, Madness, Despair,	GALLOWS.

This "moral and physical thermometer" predicts the effects of drinks ranging from water to gin. Dix advocated temperance, adamant that people control their behavior and not give in to the temptation of drink.

but he could not make the committee accept her memorial. The committee did not allow Dix to present evidence to support her claims. Instead, it based its findings on testimony by the Worcester hospital superintendent and the committee's own knowledge. Reformers decided to push to expand the Worcester facility instead of lobbying for a new mental hospital.

Dix was not a passive witness to this assault on her ideals. Showing the same determination that drove her across Massachusetts, she refused to change a word of her memorial and aggressively fought for her cause. Dix had mental hospital superintendents from all around New England write letters supporting a new asylum, and she went to the legislature's debates. Anne Heath was surprised at Dix's sudden political bravery, writing that she could "almost envy your ability to furnish yourself with engrossing, useful employment." And Dix's old acquaintance the author Lydia Maria Francis Child reported in the *National Anti-Slavery Standard* that Dix had overcome "her fastidious propriety, and almost excessive reserve of character."

In the end, the legislature barely passed a bill to enlarge the Worcester hospital by 150 beds, bringing the total number of residents to 400. Her bid to build a new asylum had failed, but Dix had found her calling.

Dix had finished her work in Massachusetts. Now, she was determined to save people with mental illness everywhere from chains, cellars, and despair. Dix set off on her own, and spent the next six months touring hospitals, jails, almshouses, and schools throughout New England and eastern Canada. As she began to travel outside Massachusetts, the "incurably" mentally ill were still Dix's chief concern. Though she did believe that mental illness could be cured if "moral treatment" was begun shortly after symptoms began, Dix thought that it was more important to concentrate on helping people with mental illness become calm than to worry about helping them regain reason and logical thought. Soon, her priorities would change.

Dix quickly set to work in Rhode Island. Her approach to millionaire Cyrus Butler was a typical example of her efforts. She learned that Butler had the money to build an asylum, but had a reputation for keeping his savings to himself. Dix went to his home and patiently told the story of Abram Simmons, a particularly pathetic prisoner in Little Compton, Rhode Island, who was confined to a dungeon. Butler immediately donated $40,000, and Providence's Butler Hospital was founded—and continues to be a center of psychiatric treatment and research today.

With a summer's worth of work behind her, Dix arrived in New York in the fall of 1843 to support a hospital for the incurable mentally ill. The state had opened the New York State Lunatic Asylum in Utica, but it was unfinished and could house just 225 patients; 2,300 mentally ill state residents were counted in the 1840 census. Worse still, the Utica hospital admitted only patients who showed the best prospects for moral treatment—victims who had fallen ill within the past two years. People with longer-term illness were left in almshouses.

Dix toured 60 counties in 10 weeks. In mid-November, she wrote to her friend George Emerson that "the travelling has been indescribably bad, chiefly plunging through mud-sloughs in mud-wagons or lumber wagons—or breaking roads through snow-drifts in *sleds*: all sorts of weather except sunny skies. I journey day and night. . . . I encounter nothing which a determined will, created by the necessities of the cause I advocate, does not enable me to vanquish." This was a stark reversal for a woman who could not walk in the night air to attend Channing's Sunday school meetings.

Dix's findings were mixed. Whereas some almshouses concealed dank cellars and chains, others were comfortable enough that Dix could "almost forget here the defects of the general system, so excellent are the domestic arrangements," as she wrote to Emerson. Dix decided to change her approach to writing.

There were no wrenching scenes in the report Dix submitted to the New York legislature in January 1844. Instead, she gave short descriptions of each county's facilities for the "insane" poor. Dix also spent more time on policy recommendations than before, explaining that mental illness was partly caused by the U.S. government. She wrote, "Insanity is . . . the result of imperfect or vicious social institutions and observances . . . revolutions, party strife, unwise and capricious legislation." She also wrote that her petition was "in behalf of the *incurable insane*, who . . . are at once the most dependent and most unfortunate of human beings."

Although some almshouses seemed adequate, Dix charged that they were "*compound* and *complex* in their plans and objects," meaning that they served as homes for the

text continues on page 62

ASTONISHING TENACITY OF LIFE

Dorothea Dix's account of the suffering of Abram Simmons was published in the Providence Journal on April 10, 1844. The report helped convince millionaire Cyrus Butler to donate $40,000 to build Butler Hospital, an institution that still serves mentally ill Rhode Islanders today.

It is said that grains of wheat, taken from within the envelope of Egyptian mummies some thousand of years old, have been found to germinate and grow in a number of instances. Even toads and other reptiles have been found alive in situations where it is evident that they must have been encased for many hundreds, if not thousands, of years.

It may, however, be doubted whether any instance has ever occurred in the history of the race where the vital principle has adhered so tenaciously to the human body under such a load and complication of sufferings and tortures as in the case of Abram Simmons, an insane man, who has been confined for several years in a dungeon in the town of Little Compton, in this State. . . . His prison was from six to eight feet square, built entirely of stone—sides, roof, and floor—and entered through two iron doors, excluding both light and fresh air, and entirely without accommodation of any description for warming and ventilating. At that time the internal surface of the walls was covered with a thick frost, adhering to the stone in some places to the thickness of half an inch . . . in utter darkness, encased on every side by walls of frost, his garments constantly more or less wet, for only wet straw to lie upon, and a sheet of ice for his covering, has this most dreadfully abused man existed through the past inclement winter. His teeth must have been worn out by constant and violent chattering for such a length of time, night and day, "Poor Tom's a-cold!"

Should any persons in this philanthropic age be disposed, from motives of curiousity, to visit the place, they may rest assured that traveling is considered quite safe in that part of the country, however improbable it may seem. The people of that region profess the Christian religion, and it is even said that they have adopted some forms and ceremonies which they call worship. It is not probable, however, that they address themselves to poor Simmons's God. Their worship, mingling with the prayers of agony which he shrieks forth from his dreary abode, would make strange discord in the ear of that Almighty Being, in whose keeping sleeps the vengeance due to all his wrongs.

This drawing of Butler Hospital is from around 1847, shortly after it was built.

elderly, sick, and orphans, as well as desperately poor residents. No single institution could care for all these groups at once, Dix argued, and people with mental illness would be much better off in an asylum designed for their needs.

Unfortunately, Dix was a threat to the very people who were most interested in new mental hospitals—asylum doctors. During the 1840s, physicians were worried that they could lose control of mental hospitals. Dix's emphasis on incurable cases embarrassed physicians. Medical treatments at the time were generally ineffective, and many experts thought doctors should not be treating mental illness at all. Why should a man who cures coughs and boils be expected to help a person who screams day and night? Moral treatment required patience from teachers like Dix, not drugs and bloodletting.

Amariah Brigham, the medical superintendent of the Utica mental hospital, fought Dix's work. No one could say for sure that a patient would not recover, he reasoned, and patients would never recover without medical treatment, he later wrote in the *American Journal of Insanity*. Brigham recruited many legislators to his cause, leading one delegate to declare that an asylum for the incurable mentally ill would be "a mad-house—a mad poorhouse—a den of filth and misery, and an object of abhorrence and disgust." Ultimately, the legislature defeated Dix's proposal for a new asylum and even rejected a resolution to thank her for her work. New York's mentally ill patients who did not have the good luck to be admitted to the Utica mental hospital were left to languish in county almshouses

By then, it was April 1844—spring, and Dix was ready to begin a new battle. She set out for Pennsylvania, where the legislature had approved a state asylum in 1840, only to have the governor veto it for financial reasons. This time, Dix was careful to approach mental hospital superintendents and ask for their support.

Dix was welcomed wherever she went, in part because her reputation as a charitable reformer was spreading.

Pennsylvanians began demanding that she write about their institutions for newspapers, make speeches, and help settle squabbles. She wrote to a friend, "I am asked to interpose between physicians and Trustees— between Wardens Chaplains and Managers—between the public and the establishments." These projects began to distract her from her asylum work, as she wrote in the same letter: "I do not see how I shall get through this state by January with all the talking and writing I have to do."

Dix worked feverishly to get to all 58 Pennsylvania counties. In late October Dix received a letter from a resident of Salem, New Jersey, protesting the state legislature's failure to found a public asylum. Dix could not resist this sort of invitation, and swept through 29 New Jersey almshouses and jails in November 1844. She finally stopped in Philadelphia in December, where she wrote her memorials for both the Pennsylvania and New Jersey state legislatures.

Applying her hard lessons from New York, Dix packed the new memorials with praise for modernity and medicine. The states had fallen "*behind* the age," while "a new

The State Lunatic Asylum in Utica, New York, was the site of one of Dix's early struggles. Dix lost the battle to provide people with "incurable' mental illness treatment here.

era has dawned on this department of medical science." She went on to describe "insanity" the same way doctors of the time would—as a "physical disease affecting and disturbing the natural and healthful functions of the brain" that was caused by a "lesion of the brain, or organic malconstruction." Mental illness could be cured with early treatment, Dix wrote, and asylums would save the state money. As Dix put it, "There is then but one alternative—condemn your needy citizens to become the life-long victims of a terrible disease, or provide remedial care in a State Hospital."

Dix urged the states to hire superintendents with medical training. She had not abandoned moral treatment, but she now conceded that doctors should prescribe it. By giving the asylums over to doctors, Dix was letting go of her belief that spiritual peace was more important than a cure for mental illness. Now, the victims were no longer sinners who needed to heal their relationship with God: They were just sick. Their emotions and desires were the by-products of illness and could be safely ignored.

Dix submitted her memorials to the New Jersey legislature on January 23, 1845, and to the Pennsylvania legislature on February 3. Once again, the memorials were excerpted in newspapers, and the New Jersey state legislature received dozens of petitions supporting the asylum.

Dix, the model of female charity, had an iron will that felled legislators in her path as she lobbied for the New Jersey and Pennsylvania asylum bills. Writing to her friend Harriet Hare, Dix complained, "You cannot imagine the labor of conversing and convincing. Some evenings I had at once, twenty gentlemen for three hours, *steady* conversation. Though they appeared perfectly unimpressible at first, the ice melted from their hearts." A New Jersey legislator declared, after listening to Dix for an hour and a half, "*I am convinced;* you've conquered me out and out; *I shall vote for the Hospital.* If you'll come to the House and talk there as you've done here, no man that isn't a brute can withstand you."

Once they had been "Miss Dix-ed," as one legislator put it, asylum opponents vanished. New Jersey passed its asylum bill in March 1845, and Pennsylvania did so one month later. Samuel Gridley Howe, remembering that he had refused Dix a job at the Normal School, wrote to her, "I recollect what you were then. I think of your noble career since & I say, God grant me to look back upon some three years of my life with a part of the self approval you must feel!"

Officials in New Jersey and Pennsylvania asked Dix to stay and help design their new asylums. She eagerly accepted, but she was uncomfortable with her new role. Dix wrote to George Emerson in July 1845, "You cannot exactly comprehend the inevitable anxieties that beset me in being *obliged* to act *with* others. The habit of delay, of declining responsibility, of prolonged discussion. . . . I wish the State Commissioners for the new Hospitals could be resolved into one energetic *heart*-working person." Dix quickly tired of the long, slow slog of committee work. It was time for her to go west.

At the beginning of her career as a reformer, Dix was energetic and the picture of health. She traveled the country and shrugged off illnesses that plagued her youth.

MORAL TREATMENT FOR PRISONERS

By August 1845, Dorothea Dix calculated that she had visited 500 almshouses, 300 jails, and several hospitals, traveling 10,000 miles in just three years. She wrote, "Sometimes I fancy my strength is wearing out, but then I revive from fatigue both of mind and body, in a way I do not comprehend." Constantly moving and working for a good cause invigorated Dix in a way that teaching never had.

As time went on, Dix had fewer and fewer reasons to go back to Boston. She had learned in February 1844 that her brother Charles had died on an ocean voyage to Africa, and she was never very close to Joseph. Dix's friends deeply respected her devotion to her work, but her endless travel and preoccupation with reform hurt her friendships. She wrote to Mary Torrey, "*You* are not in a poor-house or a Jail, and do not *need* me." She even accused Anne Heath of disloyalty and complained that "*you* dear Anne do not know or understand me: and this is not strange; for an intercourse so broken reveals but little of the growth and changes of character."

Dix worked hard to aid the mental hospitals she had helped found, returning to raise more money and sending a constant stream of gifts to make the patients' lives more pleasant: kaleidoscopes, musical instruments, and uplifting books—especially the collected works of William Ellery Channing. At the same time, however, Dix began to lose touch with the very people she wanted to help. When she first started her work in Massachusetts, she visited the East Cambridge Jail regularly, and spent much time during her visits reading the Bible to mentally ill inmates. After her New Jersey success, though, Dix wrote fewer and fewer letters to her friends about the actual conditions in poorhouses and prisons, and more about the "beautiful, almost holy" sight of mentally ill patients. The people she intended to help became abstractions to her. Dix had gone from being a Sunday school teacher to a famous lobbyist and reformer; she spent more time with politicians than patients. At the same time she was helping more people than she ever possibly could by personally teaching small Sunday School classes at the East Cambridge Jail.

In the summer of 1845, Dix turned her attention to prisons. It was a natural next step for her after improving asylums. Dix thought that prisoners, like the mentally ill, were victims of their own self-indulgence and lack of discipline. Whereas the "chronically insane" could aspire only to mental calm, prisoners could return to society if they developed their self-restraint by abstaining from alcohol, memorizing poetry, and performing hard manual labor.

Dix published a book entitled *Remarks on Prisons and Prison Discipline in the United States* in September 1845. At the time, citizens were debating whether to keep inmates apart from each other at all times—the "separate system"—or to gather inmates together to work and eat in silence, according to the "congregate system." Dix strongly preferred the separate system and, in her *Remarks,* claimed it was "a more direct application and exercise of Christian rule and precepts, than any other mode of prison-government."

With her book completed, Dix set off for Kentucky in November 1845 to help the Kentucky Eastern Lunatic

"I WOULD NOT HAVE THE OFFICERS BECOME PREACHERS"

Dorothea Dix's book Remarks on Prisons and Prison Discipline in the United States *was published in September 1845. In it, she outlined her theories about the moral development of prisoners.*

I would not have the officers become preachers . . . but I would have them all moral guides; and, while I would not desire to see them always, not very often, engaged in discoursing and formal lecturing, I would have all they both say and do produce an encouraging, awakening, and enlightening effect upon the prisoner. . . . The faint desire becomes quickened into a living purpose; this passes into the fixed resolve; and this creates a sentiment of self-respect. Self-respect implanted, conducts to the desire of possessing the respect and confidence of others; and through these paths grow up moral sentiments, gradually increasing and gaining strength; and, in time, there is the more profound and soul-saving sentiment of reverence for God, acknowledgment of his laws, and a truer perception of that sanctifying knowledge which causeth not to err.

TO THOSE

ENLIGHTENED AND BENEVOLENT MEN

IN THE

UNITED STATES,

WHOSE CONTINUED AND WELL DIRECTED EFFORTS HAVE PROCURED AN

ALLEVIATION OF THE MISERIES OF PRISONERS, AND WHOLESOME

REFORMS IN PRISON DISCIPLINE,

THE FOLLOWING PAGES ARE RESPECTFULLY INSCRIBED,

BY

D. L. DIX.

The dedication of Dix's Remarks on Prisons and Prison Discipline in the United States *shows her appreciation of other reformers. In the end, those "enlightened and benevolent men" decided that group housing of prisoners was better than Dix's "separate system."*

Asylum in Lexington lobby for a new building. She recalled being warned by good Kentucky citizens that "to travel here alone would certainly be to compromise my character as well as usefulness." Dix finally decided to "have full faith that after all a woman is her own best protector. Quiet manners and self-respect will command respect and sufficient attention from others." Her self-respect did not make her journey easy; writing to Emerson, Dix described Kentucky travel as "almost trackless forests, *over* mountains and *through* rivers. Often the way has led through a wilderness, traced by slight cuts on the trees, and houses at intervals of fourteen and twenty miles if those can be called houses which frequently consist only of a single room constructed of logs." Dix was much changed since her fainting-on-the-couch days.

Dix traveled to 44 Kentucky counties, but she did not really try to survey the entire state. Kentucky provided "out-of-door" relief, meaning that the state paid patients' relatives to support them at home. It was far more difficult for Dix to uncover abuses in private homes than in public institutions, where she could arrive unannounced.

In January 1846, Dix submitted a review of Kentucky prisons and an appeal for a new mental hospital to the state legislature. She did not request any facilities for people with incurable mental illness. Dix had abandoned her original intentions in favor of asking for the hospitals that states would actually build: hospitals that were intended to cure mental illness, not merely house incurable patients in a safe, peaceful place.

Dix claimed that people with mental illness suffered from "the mistaken tenderness within the family circle." According to Dix, these kind family members would not help the illness, and could only make the patient more excited and uncontrollable. "The solemn duty of the removal . . . of the insane . . . [from] their intimate friends and family, and their familiar homes," was necessary for a cure, according to Dix.

Recovery was certain, as "all experience shows that insanity *seasonably treated is as certainly curable as a cold or a fever*." The legislature voted for only a $5,000 allotment but did set up a committee to find a site for a new mental hospital.

Dix then meandered south, visiting institutions in Louisiana, Mississippi, Alabama, Georgia, South Carolina, Arkansas, and Missouri. She returned to Springfield, Illinois, to support a new asylum and a penitentiary. At 10 pages, the Illinois asylum memorial was Dix's shortest work yet. Dix worked with doctors from Illinois College, and the legislature quickly succumbed to Dix's lobbying.

Dix's prison work in Illinois was less successful. Submitted to the Illinois legislature on February 5, 1847, her remarks on the Alton State Penitentiary were lengthy and severe. She wrote, "*no outlay of money can convert this prison into a secure, commodious, or durable establishment*," and demanded a new building. The legislature voted to merely repair the penitentiary.

Dix was lucky that the legislature wanted to give any money to the penitentiary at all. As one state warden put it in a letter to Dix, "The people of this State manifest little or no interest in the well-being or well-doing of the men they send to their state-prison." A few years later, Illinois built a new penitentiary in Joliet—and put the congregate system into practice. Dix never broached prison reform with a state legislature again.

The Louisiana legislature approved money for an asylum the same month that Illinois did. Both the Lousiana and Illinois legislatures approved asylum funds in March 1847. Dix was pleased with her work, and reported to Anne Heath, "I grow more content with my own lot." In the summer of 1847, she took a few weeks to visit Newport and Boston, meeting the Channings, the Emersons, the Hares, and Anne Heath for the first time in years. Anne Heath wistfully wrote, "I know nothing will keep you, but wanting the power to go."

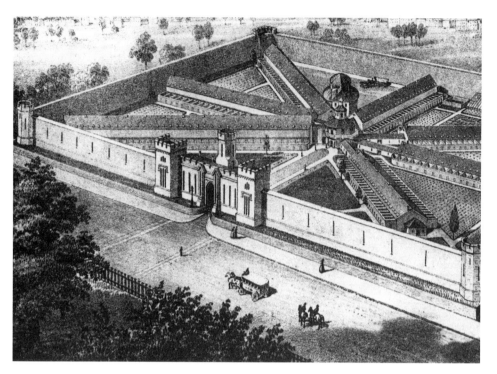

Pennsylvania's Eastern Penitentiary was a showplace for the "separate system" of solitary confinement. Dix thought that solitude would help prisoners regain self-control and return to society more quickly than group imprisonment.

In October Dix set off to lobby for improvement of the Lunatic Asylum of Tennessee, opened in 1840. Dix was no longer an unknown schoolteacher battling wardens over coal stoves; now that she was a celebrated activist, her work was much easier. Before she even arrived, the *Nashville Republican Banner* commanded residents to honor Dix and "do something worthy of her character and the age in which we live."

Dix set to work without traveling outside Nashville, the capital, and composed a memorial in just four days. The legislature printed 4,000 copies in November 1847. In response, 25 wealthy Nashville women, filled with "admiration of her disinterested, and persevering philanthropy, so honorable to their sex," asked Dix to allow a sculptor to create "in a permanent and pleasing form a countenance expressive at once, of feminine delicacy and heroic firmness, sensibility and strength, compassion and courage." Dix refused, but praised female benevolence, writing, "To us, women, it peculiarly belongs to reveal in its holiest aspects the spirituality of Religion, to bring consolations upon the troubled earth."

By the end of February, the state legislature had agreed to fund a new mental hospital designed with "the most recent and accepted plans." It was to be called a "hospital for the insane," not an "asylum," to show that it was dedicated to curing the mentally ill, not merely housing them. The legislature even passed a resolution stating that Dix's "disinterested benevolence, sublime charity, and unmixed philanthropy, challenge alike the gratitude and admiration of our State"—while granting only half the money Dix had requested. Dix was preparing for larger battles, however, and arrived in Washington, D.C., on May 15, 1848.

When Dix arrived in Washington, she told Harriet Hare, "My objects and aims now reach the length and breadth of the union." Unfortunately, during the next six years Dix would discover that the "union" was being torn apart by East-West rivalries, the question of whether to extend slavery to new territories, and debates about what rights the federal government had over the states in the first place.

After years of confronting miserly state legislatures that sent citizens to almshouses instead of hospitals, Dix had a national plan. She would fund moral treatment nationwide with the one resource the federal government had in abundance: land. The U.S. General Land Office reported in 1848 that the federal government held title to almost one billion acres of land in the states and territories.

All this land amounted to free money for whoever managed to get to it first. Dix's proposal was simple. The U.S. government would set aside five million acres of land, giving a share to each state. The states would sell their land grants to the public, then use the money to set up permanent funds to care for poor residents with mental illnesses. States would be required to use their moneys on public hospitals, not almshouses, jails, private hospitals, or new construction.

Congress had always set aside ¹⁄₁₆th of public lands for public schools, and tiny parcels of land were granted by Congress for institutions for deaf-mutes in Connecticut and Kentucky in 1819 and 1826. Still, Congress had never set aside land for charity on a national scale. At a time when there was no welfare, Social Security, or other federal programs for the needy, Dix was creating a new national commitment to the poor. Unfortunately, Dix's plan seemed to benefit older northeastern states at the expense of new territories. There was little federally owned land in New England, which had the most people and the most hospitals.

The two major political parties, the Whigs and the Democrats, had very different views of Dix's bill. The Whigs believed that the federal government should develop the country by using public land sales to fund construction of roads, canals, and other state projects. By contrast, the Democrats argued that Congress did not have the authority to use money for the states' "internal improvements." They wanted Congress just to sell federal lands at a cheap price so that Americans could develop their country. Dix's challenge was to convince Democrats that her land bill was a good idea.

Dix composed a memorial to Congress in June 1848. She had traveled more than 60,000 miles, to all but three states, and had concluded that more than 90 percent of mentally ill citizens needed help. "I have myself seen *more than nine thousand idiots, epileptics, and insane, in these United States, destitute of appropriate care and protection,*" Dix declared. This time, she emphasized the role of the state in *creating* mental illness. As she had done in the New York memorial, Dix explained that the pressures of competition in a democracy lead to mental illness because "every individual, however obscure, is free to enter upon the race for the highest honors and most exalted stations." The idea that American political freedom caused mental illness was common at the time, but Dix's solution was original. The federal government, she said, had a duty to cure victims of mental illness because they were *"wards of the nation"* and not the responsibility of state governments alone.

Dix found a sponsor for her bill in John Adams Dix (no relation), a Democratic senator from New York. On June 27, 1848, Senator Dix read portions of the memorial to the Senate, and he moved to have the subject studied by a new committee. By the end of the session in August, though, Dix's bill was buried by factional feuds and opposition from southern and western states.

Dix was determined to reintroduce the bill during Congress's winter session. In the meantime, she left for North Carolina. Although she spent years in Washington, she made use of every recess to travel and support asylum bills. Over the next few years, Dix swept through the South, lobbying and inspecting almshouses as she went.

Back in Washington in January 1849, Dix discovered that Congress was at a standstill. James K. Polk was a lame-duck President, with only three months left before the March inauguration of Zachary Taylor, and Congress was unsure what new policies Taylor would bring to the White House. Settlers and speculators were charging to California for the 1849 gold rush, and Congress urgently needed to settle the question of whether slavery would be extended to the territory. Dix's bill was ignored that session.

Dix made herself busy. She met with members of Congress and wrote letters. On Sundays, she visited the

Senator John A. Dix was a Democrat who opposed extending slavery to the territories, and could not get Dix's land grant bill passed.

District of Columbia penitentiary and donated morally uplifting books to the prison library. Still, she was not content. Writing to her brother Joseph, she grumbled that although "I certainly enjoy all the advantages any one can possess here in relation to social position and public favor . . . life in Washington is very tedious and very annoying."

Refusing to be idle while Congress was in recess, Dix traveled through the deep South during the winter of 1849–50. She had not become sympathetic to the struggle to end slavery. Writing to her brother Joseph the previous year, she reaffirmed her opinions from St. Croix that the slaves were "gay, obliging, and anything but miserable." Dix also charged that they had no self-discipline, calling them "thoughtless and irresponsible." By contrast, the mentally ill poor had her sympathy because they could not control their own behavior. Like most of her fellow Northerners, she saw the fight as mere political pettiness. She raged to Harriet Hare in February 1850, "I have *no* patience and no sympathy either with northern Abolitionists or southern agitators. I am quite sure that neither the one nor the other party would willingly see the question of Slavery determined as in that case they would lose the whole political capital which they possess or are likely to command."

While Dix was on the road, her old friend Horace Mann, now a Massachusetts Congressman, wrote in May 1850 to tell her that "it cannot be of the least service for you to be here until this all-absorbing question of the Territories is [settled] unless you can work miracles. If you can bring that power, come any time." Dix arrived within days and learned that Mann was correct. As Congress argued over the territories, Dix chaperoned her bill from committee to committee, making sure that it stayed far from the debates. Instead of trying to win over western legislators by changing how the lands would be selected, Dix relied on her personal influence on legislators, believing that her moral will would win out.

This time, Dix chose Democratic representative William Bissell of Illinois and Whig senator James A. Pearce of Maryland to sponsor her bill. They dutifully introduced it in late June, but the unending slavery debates kept the bill—and almost all other legislation—from coming to the floor. The wrangling stopped in August. With the sudden death of President Zachary Taylor in July, Whig Vice President Millard Fillmore came into office. Dix was ecstatic. Fillmore was a Unitarian, and she had become friends with him and his family over the summer.

Fillmore signed two compromise bills in mid-September. California would be a free state, while the New Mexico and Utah territories would decide on slavery themselves. Congress was finally ready to tackle land distribution. Dix's bill came to the floor of the Senate on September 26.

Senator Jefferson Davis, who later became the president of the Confederacy, claimed that the government was merely a trustee over that land and therefore could not authorize Dix's bill. More ominously, Democrat David Rice Atchison of Missouri argued that the bill was unfair to the western states. The eastern states, which had no federal lands in their borders, would get a share of the new, valuable lands in the territories, while the western states would be stuck trying to unload the worthless land still unsold inside their borders. Dix had failed to change her bill to suit the western senators, and it died quietly.

Congress began a new session in December 1850. The Senate approved the re-introduced bill, and on February 18, Bissell had the House of Representatives call for a vote. Unfortunately, states' rights Democrats introduced dozens of parliamentary procedures to waste time, until Whig representative George Ashmun of Massachusetts declared, "I have voted as long as I think it expedient for Miss Dix, and I desire the bill to pass; but I think we ought first to attend to more important public business." The bill was abandoned.

Dix would be back for the 32nd Congress of 1852; in the meantime, her files were bursting with letters from asylum advocates around the country, pleading for her help. She journeyed through South Carolina, Georgia, and Florida, sending reports back to her friend President Fillmore. In one letter to him, she commented, "All the bombast, declamation and legislation touching secession [is] just the passing ebullition of passionate politicians and excitable men who had really no great influence." Still, she was personally affected. Arriving in a small town where there were rumors that abolitionists were planning to lead a slave revolt, Dix found that "*every person* avoided *even looking towards me. It was really quite odd.*" This sort of uncivil behavior made Dix angry. She began writing to friends about the "vicious machinations of Abolitionists" and asserted it was clear "that the people have serious ground of complaint against the unjustifiable proceedings of northern unprincipled abolitionists."

Millard Fillmore served as President of the United States from 1850 to 1854. A personal friend of Dix, he shared her Unitarian faith.

Dix returned to Washington to find the Whigs had shrunk to a minority of the House. She occupied herself by writing yet another memorial, this time to replace a psychiatric hospital in Maryland. Her national bill came out of committee in August 1852 with an amendment giving grants from territories to any state that had federal lands that could not be sold for $1.25 an acre—the "worthless" lands that had worried Senator Atchison. Dix was not pleased with the amendment; it seemed like a trivial issue to her and another excuse for senators to argue her bill to death. But it satisfied the bill's western opponents, and the House of Representatives passed the measure.

The amended bill now headed to the Senate, and Dix became anxious. She asked New York Whig senator William H. Seward to *"Please*, please, rouse *all your friends* to finish the work now *wisely* and *well*. Please pass it *at once."* Unfortunately, the bill sank when the Senate refused to vote on it, thanks to last-minute amendments for railroad subsidies, among other items, attached to it. With her bill defeated once again, Dix stayed in the capital to set up a psychiatric hospital. Congress had earlier passed financing for the project in August 1852, creating what is now St. Elizabeth's Hospital in Washington, D.C.

Men are taken to an asylum in Dublin. When Dix visited Ireland in 1854, the potato famine and other ills had left Irish institutions overburdened.

A Veto at Home, a Welcome in Europe

In the summer of 1853, newly elected President Franklin Pierce, a Democrat, made appointments to his cabinet. Dorothea Dix's most passionate opponent, Jefferson Davis, became secretary of war. She had gone from chatting with her friend and fellow Unitarian, President Fillmore to being an outsider at Pierce's White House.

Dix prepared for another long siege when the 33rd Congress began in December 1853. She wrote to Anne Heath, "God, I think, will surely give me strength for *His* work so long as he directs my line of duty." She met with Pierce on December 7 and wrote to Millard Fillmore about "that air of restless, half uncertainty he [Pierce] wears," and she described their encounter. When Dix asked Pierce if her reintroduced bill would receive his "interest and good will," Pierce replied offhandedly, "I shall be glad if it passes now, but I really have not gone into the subject." Dix was not reassured by this extremely weak endorsement of her bill.

Her bill needed more than good will. It cleared the Senate committee on Public Lands on the same day that a bill to reorganize the Nebraska Territory was reintroduced by Democratic senator Stephen A. Douglas. Douglas wanted to repeal the Missouri Compromise, which prohibited slavery north of the 36°30' latitude, and let the settlers—not the federal government—decide whether slavery would be legal in the Nebraska Territory. This legislation was called the Kansas-Nebraska Bill because the territory was to be divided into two states, and it quickly became a test of Democratic Party loyalty.

By then, Dix was nervous about her bill. The opening of the Nebraska Territory meant that there would be even more bills granting land to railroads than before, and Douglas's proposal was creating demand for a homestead bill to give settlers free farms. Dix wrote to Fillmore, "Either the whole public domain will be disposed of at *random*, or all Land Bills, my own included, will be crushed."

In reality, Democrats were eager to vote for Dix's bill, but not because of her lobbying. A rumor was spreading through Congress that President Pierce would veto the bill. A veto would give Pierce an opportunity to explain his position on land grants in general—a position that the Democrats were eager to learn—and would give northern, southern, and western Democrats a clear position they could all support. After bitter fighting over slavery in the Nebraska Territory, the party was desperate to find a common cause.

Dix's bill was approved by the Senate and went to

President Franklin Pierce vetoed Dix's land grant bill, effectively destroying the movement for national funding of mental hospitals.

a vote in the House on April 19, 1854. Representative Thomas Clingman of North Carolina managed to comment on Dix's Bill, the homesteaders, and the Kansas-Nebraska Bill all at once: "This Government has no authority, under the powers given to it as a Federal and limited Government, to legislate in this way for either the lunatics, paupers, negroes, or anybody else." Still, the bill passed, 81 to 53. Dix did not celebrate. She wrote to Anne Heath on April 28, "As yet the President has not put his Veto upon my Bill, but I fully expect it today or in a few days—and poor, weak man, it will be a bad day's work for him." She continued, "A storm impends which *he* little dreams of. It will shake his very life."

Pierce returned his veto on May 3. Arguing that mentally ill patients were not the only needy Americans, Pierce dismissed "the novel and vast field of legislation" that the bill required; he was not willing to set up a welfare state. Pierce also argued that the federal government could not use its power over the territories for any national goal, because the government was merely a trustee of the lands. Pierce did note that railroads were consistent with good trusteeship, because they increased the value of territories' property.

Dix wrote that the veto "fell on my spirits like a weight of ice." Then she got busy. She lobbied her friends in Congress to override the veto and calculated that a coalition of half the Senate Democrats and all of the Whigs would provide the necessary two-thirds majority. She told Anne Heath, "In the abstract game of Chess I am waging with the President thus far I hold all the advantage." Dix underestimated her opponents. Congress had only overridden one veto in the history of the country. At a time when the Democratic party was struggling for unity, congressional Democrats were loathe to oppose their President.

Newspapers had mixed opinions about Dix's bill and what it showed about Dix's character as a woman. The Whiggish *Baltimore American* stated that the bill would be proof of Dix's true womanly charity and benevolence "when the last remembrance of the disputatious women who thrust themselves into the arena of public life and contend with loud-mouthed volubility for rights that would unsex and disgrace them shall have passed away, and the world has forgotten even to contemn them." In Virginia, the *Richmond Enquirer* saw the bill as a drastic extension of federal control, disguised as legislation "originating in the crotchet of a crazy old woman."

For two months, the Senate debated the veto off and on, touching on the Kansas-Nebraska question, federal power, and previous land grants. Dix waited and hoped. On July 6, 1854, the Senate finally voted to sustain the veto, 27 to 24, with only four Democrats joining the Whigs. Dix had failed. Still, her bill had helped Democrats unite to repeal the ban on slavery in the new states and territories. In a small way, Dorothea Dix had helped to begin the crisis that would lead to the Civil War.

In a letter to her friend Senator Charles Sumner of Massachusetts, Dix raged at congressmen who were "so false to their own *previously declared opinions* and *principles* as to vote within one month *four times*, alternating on each occasion as the Vane on the neighboring Engine House." No one else seemed to react to the sustained veto. The public failed to cry out for mental hospitals, and the Senate quickly turned to reducing public land prices.

Dix left Washington in August 1854 and contemplated what to do with her life. "I betake myself to the do-nothing class," she wrote to Anne Heath, lamenting that "the poor weak President has by an unprecedented extremity of folly lacerated my life." Dix decided to revisit the one home she never wanted to leave—Greenbank. In September, she set off for Liverpool.

After arriving at Greenbank, Dix wrote to Anne Heath, "I have not the *slightest interest* in going into France, nor even Italy. In contrast with the aim of my accustomed pursuits it seems the most trivial use of time." She noted that in Britain, "I can travel *alone* without difficulty, which would be out of the question to attempt *on the Continent*."

Although Dix claimed that she went to Europe to relax, before she left she had taken the time to get a letter of introduction to the chief British mental health reformer, Anthony Ashley Cooper, Earl of Shaftesbury. In 1845 Shaftesbury had proposed successful legislation in Parliament that required each county in England and Wales to create a mental hospital, and established a national Commission on Lunacy to oversee the hospitals, which he chaired. Shaftesbury was delighted that Dix would be aiding the cause. One of Shaftesbury's goals was to extend the county hospital law to Scotland.

Dix began her travels in an area where Shaftesbury's laws did not apply: Ireland. She spent October 1854 inspecting Irish prisons, poorhouses, hospitals, and schools, and she was unimpressed—perhaps more by the people than the institutions. During the potato famine of 1845–46, perhaps a million Irish men, women, and children had died of starvation when the potato crop was ruined by a blight; thousands of the survivors had immigrated to the United States. Dix wrote to Anne Heath that the Irish were "sorely degraded by a thousand causes, and *we* reap the curse of a vicious population sent over to people our now fast corrupted and overburthened country."

Dix was more impressed by the Scottish mental hospitals when she began traveling there in January 1855. Scotland's major cities had Royal Asylums, model institutions like St. Elizabeth's in Washington, D.C. Unfortunately, many of Scotland's poor patients lived in private asylums, which were often run on tiny town budgets by keepers who did not offer any treatment. Patients were sometimes shackled to the walls. Dix wrote to friends in February 1855, "I really cannot with a quiet conscience leave Britain till these abominable places are broken up or controlled."

In Edinburgh Dix pressed her views upon the Scottish medical establishment. Repeating the claim of American asylum superintendents, Dix said private asylums were horrible because doctors did not supervise them. Most of the medical community in Edinburgh agreed with her, but one physician called her "the American invader." This doctor, W. A. F. Browne, with his Royal Asylum colleagues, worried that a new Scottish commission on lunacy would gain control of the Royal Institutions, destroying doctors' independence.

On February 26, Dix learned that one of her opponents was leaving for London the next day to lobby against her reforms. She jumped on an overnight mail train and rushed from the train station to meet with the Duke of Argyll, a friend of Shaftesbury's, to ask him to speak to the Home Secretary for the new commission. Dix managed to persuade the lord advocate for Scotland in Parliament to endorse a new Scottish Lunacy Commission and returned to Scotland. Upon returning to Edinburgh, Dix realized that "*I have done my part*," as she wrote to Elizabeth Rathbone.

Dix was invigorated. She canceled her trip back to the United States; Europe was more interesting than she had hoped. Dix promised Elizabeth Rathbone that she would "forswear all hospitals & hospital thoughts," and "glide up & down the Rhine lazily," but she carried in her trunk the addresses of Dutch physicians and asylums and a letter of introduction to the king of Holland from a Dutch doctor. She left London on August 6 to meet the Rathbones in Antwerp, Belgium. With the Rathbones, she journeyed from Belgium to the Alps.

Dix, awed by nature, found the Alps brought "the highest most spiritual happiness I ever enjoyed," as she later wrote. After returning with the Rathbones to Liverpool in October, Dix decided to do more traveling, this time with American physician Joseph Parrish and his wife to Paris, to inspect French mental hospitals.

Although the French government generously supported its mental hospitals, Dix found that Parisian hospitals had

many "radical universal defects," such as too little ventilation, as she reported to Maria Bottolph. Dix was not fond of the city, either. The bright lights, the theater, ballet, and other arts did not interest her at all. She wrote to Bottolph, "I cannot imagine *what* constitute its so binding attractions to the many who resort thither."

The Arc de Triomphe dominates the Avenue des Champs Elysées in Paris. Dix was not at all impressed by the city.

While the hospitals displeased Dix, she was delighted to discover that her old friend George Emerson was in Paris. Tiring of Joseph Parrish, Dix insisted that the Emersons move to her hotel. She went on excursions with them and met them in the evenings after she toured charitable institutions. By the end of their Paris stay, the Emersons were tired of her. Writing home to his daughter, George Emerson complained, "We have the advantage of seeing Dolly every day, who knows every thing. You may conceive of her penetration."

Later, while traveling alone through Italy, Dix inspected the Santo Spirito mental hospital in Rome and concluded

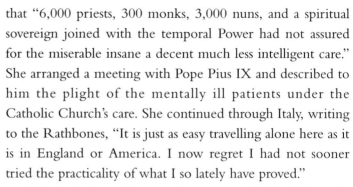

that "6,000 priests, 300 monks, 3,000 nuns, and a spiritual sovereign joined with the temporal Power had not assured for the miserable insane a decent much less intelligent care." She arranged a meeting with Pope Pius IX and described to him the plight of the mentally ill patients under the Catholic Church's care. She continued through Italy, writing to the Rathbones, "It is just as easy travelling alone here as it is in England or America. I now regret I had not sooner tried the practicality of what I so lately have proved."

Dix had planned to continue on to Holland, but she changed her plans when she had a chance to travel to Turkey. In February 1856, Russia, Britain, France, and Turkey had met in the Congress of Paris to end the Crimean War, which had been raging on the coast of the Black Sea since 1853. Dix was never particularly interested in the war, but she *was* interested in Florence Nightingale, and she hoped to meet her in Turkey.

Florence Nightingale, the model of Victorian female benevolence, transformed filthy wards into sanitary hospitals during the Crimean War. Dix repeatedly tried to meet her, but missed her each time.

As the British Government's "Superintendent of the Female Nurses in the Hospitals in the East," Nightingale had arrived at the filthy Barrack Hospital in Scutari, Turkey, where soldiers lay on straw mattresses on a floor splattered with mud, blood, vomit, and urine, and she transformed it into a sanitary place for healing. Called the "Lady with the Lamp" by soldiers who saw her tending to them on her nightly rounds of the wards, Nightingale was the epitome of English female charity.

Dix set off for Constantinople (now called Istanbul) in her typical way. She simply walked onto a steamship in Venice. As she boasted to a friend, "I take no refusals, and yet I speak neither Italian, German, Greek or Slavonic. I have *no* letters of Introduction, and know no persons en route." Arriving in Turkey on April 10, Dix jumped into a small ferryboat and barked "Hospital! Scutari!" The ferrymen obliged and rowed Dix to Scutari in a half an hour.

With help from a British sailor, Dix found the hospital and strode into the ward. Unfortunately, Dix's self-reliance had thwarted her. Nightingale, unaware that she would be having a guest, had left for a British hospital at Balaklava across the Black Sea a few weeks earlier. Dix inspected the hospital anyway and found that it was in good order.

Disappointed by failing to meet Nightingale, Dix turned back toward the West. Leaving Europe, she could reflect on her successes. The Scottish commission had recommended that the government establish public mental hospitals and a commission to ensure medical supervision of all mental hospitals. She had word that the pope would improve conditions for Rome's patients. Perhaps her accomplishments in Europe made up for the demise of her land-grant bill. Dix left for the United States on September 17, 1856, promising the Rathbones that she would be back to celebrate their golden wedding anniversary in 1862. She never returned.

Dix (top left), Florence Nightingale (lower right), and other women reformers are featured in this issue of Godey's Lady's Book, *a popular women's magazine.*

8

A MODEL OF CHARITY FOR THE SOUTH

When Dix arrived from Europe, the United States was boiling with war fever. While Dix was still in Europe, her friend Charles Sumner was beaten unconscious on the Senate floor by a cane-wielding South Carolina congressman during a heated debate over the Kansas-Nebraska Bill.

The Whig party had collapsed as Northern members joined the new Republican party or the antislavery Free Soil party and Southern Whigs fled to the Democrats. Democrat James Buchanan won the 1856 Presidential election, and Dix blamed the result on the voters' character flaws, grumbling to Fillmore, "The masses are too ignorant, the educated too busy, too self-seeking or too procrastinating to heed the real facts of our National position."

Dix saw that there was no hope for her national land bill, and at the state level, she had worked herself out of a job. Thanks to her efforts and the larger asylum movement, most states had at least one hospital for the mentally ill. Thousands of Americans were now living in state mental hospitals, many for years at a time.

By 1856 it was becoming clear that moral treatment could not cure most of the people at these mental hospitals,

SOUTHERN CHIVALRY — ARGUMENT versus CLUB'S.

In this cartoon, Senator Charles Sumner is beaten unconscious on the Senate floor by South Carolina congressman Preston Brooks after Sumner made a speech opposing slavery. The attack heightened tensions between the North and the South.

however. Instead, they stayed there while new patients kept moving in. By the late 1850s, more than half of the inmates at the Worcester hospital had been "insane" for more than five years. At other institutions, superintendents estimated that less than a third of their patients had any chance of recovery. Dix's well-ordered communities were becoming crowded, chaotic places, some housing twice as many patients as they had been designed to hold. Some mental hospitals were abandoning moral treatment altogether, substituting the shackles and restraints that had horrified Dix in the almshouses.

Dix blamed the patients, claiming that asylums were failing because of the flood of Irish immigrants, who simply did not respond to moral treatment. She simply assumed that the Irish were inferior people and prone to mental illness, as she had when she visited Ireland. Dix's views on immigrants were typical for her time. The "Know-Nothing" political party, devoted to limiting Irish and

German Catholic immigration to protect the power of native-born Protestant Americans, flourished in the 1850's and won 21 percent of the vote in the 1856 Presidential election. When she was not working for the good of the poor, Dix's views were politically conservative.

Dix traveled to New York in December 1856 to support the construction of two new asylums, and then to Germantown, Pennsylvania, to help lobby for funds for a school for mentally retarded children. The Pennsylvania school got its funds, but the New York assembly rejected the bill for two new asylums.

In May 1857, the Scottish commission's report on private asylums scandalized Parliament, which passed the Lunatic Asylums (Scotland) Act of 1857, creating a network of public mental hospitals there. The *New York Journal of Commerce* announced on June 20, "Miss Dix deserves to be at least as much honored in the United States for her beneficent and arduous explorations in Europe, as Miss Nightingale is in Great Britain for her enterprise and hospital services in the Crimea." During the summer of 1857, Dix spent time at Oakland. Her friends Ruth Channing, Sarah Gibbs, and Harriet Hare were almost 80 years old, and Dix enjoyed the sunny days with them.

In late September, Dix rushed to Boston to aid Anne Heath, who was struck by typhoid fever. Dix kept Heath up far into the night, talking and talking. Heath's sister Susan wrote in her diary that Dix "had no *mercy* on her—but would certainly kill her or drive her distracted." After Dix left, Heath became severely ill before recovering.

Perhaps Dix was trying to bridge the gap between them. Heath had lived quietly in Brookline, Massachusetts, all her life and was close to her family. Though she had never married, in 1858 Heath was caring for her 16-year-old niece, Grace, and sharing her joys and sorrows. By contrast, Dix traveled so much that she had no real home and little contact with family members, and she avoided Boston as much as she could. Fifty-six-year-old Dix had no contact with young people, unless they were patients or inmates. She was welcomed all over the country; as she later wrote to Anne Heath, "There is not a Hospital . . . where I do not feel at ease and enough at home to ask for what I want and find contentment."

The country itself, however, was not contented. Dix was becoming increasingly concerned with the North-South conflict. She was determined to improve the situation by personal example, demonstrating her own self-restraint and feminine charity. In January 1859, she left for the deep South.

Dix arrived in Charleston, South Carolina, and spent two weeks raising funds to support the state mental hospital. She reported to Millard Fillmore, "The Abolition fever seems declining, and Southern Citizens may have time to improve the condition of the Negro population, if not disturbed by indiscreet northern interference."

Dix continued on to Texas, where she encountered some of the worst traveling of her life. From Houston, Dix took the train as far as the tracks had been laid and then boarded a stagecoach. For two days and nights Dix rode in the coach, spending one night at the bottom of a gully where the coach was stuck in mud. Anne Heath was horrified. "I feel as if you were going among Cannibals, and would never return. How *can* you do so! I wish you would come home . . . I wish you would stay in civilized quarters!"

Dix continued on to St. Louis. There, she met Unitarian minister William Greenleaf Eliot, who believed, like Dix, that "individual virtue" could resolve the slavery crisis, perhaps by compelling owners to free their slaves voluntarily. In Jackson, Mississippi, the legislature was friendly to her. Dix was, after all, one of the few Northerners willing to acknowledge that the Southern slave states had any good will at all. After passing a unanimous resolution

thanking Dix for her efforts, the legislature approved funding to expand the State Hospital for the Insane.

Dix returned to South Carolina in November 1859. In Columbia, Dix found that the legislature was busy debating secession. In two weeks, however, Dix convinced the lawmakers to budget $85,000 for an asylum—almost as much as South Carolina was putting aside for military preparations for the coming war. Anne Heath was impressed by Dix's powers, writing, "Surely the angels have charge concerning you. Would not any other northerner have been killed to bits, without Judge or Jury? And *you* were welcomed, listened to, and commended!"

After Dix reached Pennsylvania in January 1860, she fell ill with influenza. Just as she was confident that individual virtue could save the country, she was sure that her own willpower would heal her. Dix recovered in March and began lobbying again, which resulted in the Pennsylvania legislature's approval of $100,000 for a school for mentally retarded children and two mental hospitals. Dix reckoned

Stagecoach passengers typically got a rough ride. Dix frequently traveled by stagecoach during her tours of hospitals and prisons.

that she had obtained more than $500,000 for mental hospitals in the past two years.

By now, Dix was tired of lobbying. She told Anne Heath that "instead of exhorting people to do their duty, I shall talk less, and think & act more." Dix spent a few weeks visiting Pennsylvania institutions, but her heart was not in it. All she seemed to find was hordes of Irish immigrants in city facilities for the insane, whom Dix unfortunately dismissed with bigotry. She thought the American citizens could be cured, but wrote to Elizabeth Rathbone, "Mostly they [the immigrants] are incurable, especially the Catholics

An Irish immigrant reads an advertisement for ship passage to New York. Dix disapproved of these new immigrants, who sometimes ended up in the hospitals she founded.

who seem singularly low in intellect or dulled by their religious creed and total want of education."

Dix missed her national work and longed to have Florence Nightingale's impact on the world. She soon got a chance to act on the national scene—made possible by her friendly relations with the South. Southerners rightly saw her as sympathetic to their cause, and Dix heard many rumors unavailable to sterner moralists. In January 1861, she arrived at the Philadelphia office of Samuel Morse Felton, president of the Philadelphia, Wilmington, & Baltimore Railroad. She closed the door and explained, as Felton later put it, that there was an "extensive and organized conspiracy throughout the South" to attack Washington. Troops were practicing maneuvers along railroad tracks, preparing to assault the trains. According to Dix, the South planned to cut off all railroad traffic to Washington, assassinate Abraham Lincoln, and then "declare the Southern conspirators . . . the Government of the United States."

Felton ordered an investigation and found that everything she said was true. He made sure that Lincoln traveled to Washington secretly by overnight train, and the President-elect arrived safely two days before he was scheduled to appear. The Civil War was about to begin.

9

THE AMERICAN
FLORENCE
NIGHTINGALE

On April 19, 1861, Dorothea Dix went to the White House and volunteered to lead nurses for the Union cause. She waited patiently for two days to be given permission to start her work. The previous year, Dix had written, "The South is literally insane on the secession question." Now, she was ready to administer moral treatment to an entire nation. She had already been compared to Florence Nightingale. Dix was going to try to become America's war heroine.

On April 21, 1861, Dix sent a note to Secretary of War Simon Cameron, offering "*free service* in the Military Hospitals, for so long as shall be needed" and promising to serve "*subject to the regulations* established by the Surgical Staff." She also asked for the authority to "call in such substantial aid as I can immediately effect." In other words, Dix offered to work without pay, to submit to the supervision of doctors, and to raise money for the hospitals.

Cameron accepted Dix's offer the next day and suggested she start recruiting nurses and helping to organize and distribute supplies. Dix took on the title of Superintendent of Women Nurses and began to organize her new Office of Women Nurses. She began by consulting the acting sur-

The Women's Central Association of Relief, meeting here in 1864, organized training for Civil War nurses. These energetic women staunchly opposed Dix's policies for nurses and helped create the U.S. Sanitary Commission.

geon general, Colonel Robert C. Wood of the army's medical department. Wood was eager to please the military doctors, who generally detested women nurses. At the time, most nurses were male, and untrained. They were often recruited from among the soldiers who were hospitalized but had only minor wounds. When he spoke with Dix, Wood stressed that her first priority was to gather supplies for the army. The medical department had enough bandages, clothing, and bedding for 15,000 soldiers during peacetime but not for a war in which 30,000 men might fight in a single battle.

Dix agreed to this plan far too eagerly. She had not spent much time raising money, except from state legislatures, and did not know how to respond to Wood's demands. When he asked her to collect 500 hospital gowns two days after her appointment, Dix bought them with her own money.

Wood knew that thousands of determined Northern women would soon be descending on military hospitals, following the men to war. On May 1, he announced that all women volunteers had to report to Dix because "efficient and well-directed service can only be rendered through a systematic arrangement." It would be her job to reject and restrain volunteers.

At the same time, the Women's Central Association of Relief (WCAR) in New York was organizing women nurses for the war. Founded by Elizabeth Blackwell (the first woman to graduate from an American medical school), her younger sister (Dr. Emily Blackwell), and Dr. Maria Zakrzewska (a German émigré and doctor), the WCAR was run by young, energetic women who felt strongly that they should be included in the war effort. Unlike women of Dix's generation, the WCAR members had trained to work outside the home, and many of them had graduated from Elizabeth Blackwell's training program for nurses.

Louisa Lee Schuyler, soon to be the WCAR president, wrote to Dix to ask her opinions on volunteer nurses. Dix replied promptly and sternly, stating that the women "should by no means come on now," presumably because Dix felt that a swarm of eager volunteers would overwhelm her "systematic arrangement."

Dix went on to detail what kind of moral qualities the nurses should have, but she never specified any sort of medical training, apart from "some suitable organized instruction in nursing duties." In an unintended insult, she also wrote that "no young ladies should be sent at all," disqualifying the 24-year-old Schuyler.

On May 4 Dix published a press release repeating these requirements. There was no other publicity for recruiting women nurses—no advertisements or articles. Presumably, Dix expected to impress the North by her personal example with a few select nurses, just as Florence Nightingale had done in the Crimean War.

With the help of Unitarian minister Henry Whitney Bellows, the WCAR decided to ask the government to approve a Sanitary Commission, whose job would be to

Women serving the U.S. Sanitary Commission worked in many settings to reduce casualties from infection and to support the Union troops. Dix sparred with the Sanitary Commission and ultimately lost power over Civil War nursing.

prevent disease among the troops. This care was sorely needed; during the Mexican War of 1846–48, for every American soldier killed by battle wounds, seven had died from disease.

Bellows met with Dix in Washington on May 17. The WCAR doctors were unknown and hoped to benefit from Dix's national reputation and personal connections in Washington. Dix, too, saw the benefits of an alliance and happily backed the formation of the Sanitary Commission. On June 13, President Lincoln approved the new commission, which would advise the medical department on functions including "the proper provision of cooks, nurses, and hospitals."

Dix's relations with the new commission were tense from the start. When 28-year-old Georgeanna Woolsey, a graduate of Blackwell's nurse training program and a member of New York's wealthy social elite, arrived to inspect army hospitals for the WCAR, she stopped by a dying soldier's bedside to fan and comfort him. The doctor in charge of the hospital demanded that Woolsey stop her unauthorized care. Dix sided with the doctor and "brought all the weight of professional indignation to bear upon me," Woolsey later wrote. Dix did not believe that benevolent women should oppose the hospital's authority. Woolsey and the WCAR, however, were not prepared to obey Dix's rigid, old-fashioned rules of "femininity."

Dix's rules for nurses sounded like her old plans for the Massachusetts Normal School. One volunteer reported that women "must be in their own room at taps, or nine o' clock, unless obliged to be with the sick; must not go to any place of amusement in the evening." She also alienated women with her requirements for nurses: "No woman under thirty years need apply to serve in the government hospitals. All nurses are required to be very plain-looking women. Their dresses must be brown or black, with no bows, no curls, or jewelry, and no hoop-skirts." Dix became widely known as a foolish old woman who thought that nurses ought to be ugly.

In reality, Dix never rejected an applicant for being too attractive. She was simply worried that young women would see the war as a romantic place to find a husband. Dix also suspected that the few nurses who were individually approved by doctors were their mistresses, and she warned new nurses to be wary of advances. Dix was also kind to her volunteers. She personally welcomed nurses to Washington and frequently gave them gifts of flowers, clothes, food, or money, in part to boost the nurses' dismal pay—just as Nightingale had done for her nurses.

Unlike Nightingale, who visited each soldier's bedside at night, Dix never spent much time with patients. She never mentioned them in her letters, and a volunteer nurse complained to the *New York Times* in December 1861 that Dix "does not live in the hospitals, but in her comfortable house in Washington, and has never nursed a sick soldier, nor folded a shroud over a dead one, since the war began."

Dix quietly ignored attacks on her reputation. She continued to see herself as a private woman who acted out of benevolence, rather than a government representative, and she not only refused payment but spent all of her own money on her war work. When her friend Joseph Henry saw Dix looking "feeble and

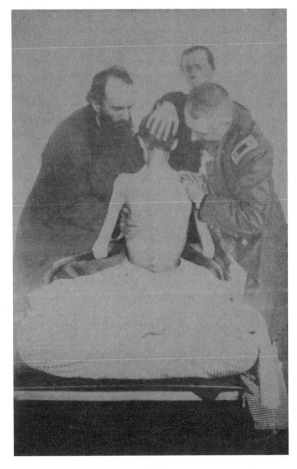

On both the Union and Confederate sides, many prisoners of war, like the soldier being examined in this photograph, suffered from starvation and disease. Dix inspected Union prisons and interviewed Union prisoners who had been released.

WAR WORK

Mary Phinney was born to a prosperous farming family in Lexington, Massachusetts. After her war work, she went on to marry a German count. Her son published her diary of her war years. In her autobiography, Adventures of an Army Nurse, *she recalls the advice of Dorothea Dix.*

Miss Dix, who had been appointed by the Resident head of the army nurses, took me from Washington to Alexandria to the Mansion House Hospital. She told me on the journey that the surgeon in charge was determined to give her no foothold in any hospital where he reigned, and that I was to take no notice of anything that might occur, and was to make no complaint whatever might happen. She was a stern woman of few words. . . . the surgical ward . . . consisted of many small rooms, with a broad corridor, every room so full of cots that it was only barely possible to pass between them. Such a sorrowful sight; the men had just been taken off the battle-field, some of them had been lying three or four days almost without clothing, their wounds never dressed, so dirty and wretched . . . soon the doctors came and ordered me to follow them while they examined and dressed the wounds. They seem to me then, and afterwards I found they were, the most brutal men I ever saw. . . . The surgeon told me he had no room for me, and a nurse told me he said he would make the house so hot for me I would not stay long. When I told Miss Dix I could not remain without a room to sleep in, she, knowing the plan of driving me out, said "My child," (I was nearly as old as herself), "you will stay where I have placed you."

exhausted," he quietly asked Secretary of War Cameron to pay for a small wagon and driver for Dix, so that she would not have to trudge through the streets in winter. Dix refused the gift, declaring "I give cheerfully my *whole* time, mind, *strength,* and *income,* to the service of my country." She continued, "Indeed I have done this for 21 years, only transferring from Hospitals for the insane the means I now render to the Military service. I cannot now begin to receive any form of remuneration for what I cheerfully render as a loyal woman."

Dix even operated her Office of Women Nurses out of her rented house. There, she greeted nurses, stored donated supplies, and provided beds for nurses who had not yet found homes. Dix had no assistants; she organized every aspect of the office by herself. The Sanitary Commission, by contrast, met in an elegant office in the U.S. Treasury Building.

These two organizations were bound to clash. Dix attended the first official meeting of the Sanitary Commission in Washington in July 1861. The commissioners were unimpressed with Dix. Writing in his diary a few weeks afterward, George Templeton Strong, a New York lawyer on the committee, termed Dix a "philanthropic lunatic" and observed that "she is energetic, benevolent, unselfish, and a mild case of monomania. . . . Working on her own hook, she does good, but no one can cooperate with her."

The Civil War was quickly turning into a long, bloody fight. At the battle of Wilson's Creek, Missouri, on August 10, 1861, the Union suffered almost 1,000 casualties. These men had to be taken 110 miles to the nearest railroad before they could be transported to a military hospital in St. Louis—a hospital so new that it had no beds or nurses. Hundreds of wounded soldiers languished in the summer heat for a week with no treatment.

Heedless of the Sanitary Commission's claim to be the sole official public health committee, John C. Frémont, the federal commander of the Western Department of the war, telegraphed Dix directly, begging her to "come here and organize these hospitals." Arriving on September 2, Dix found that local residents, including her friend William Greenleaf Eliot, had already begun organizing relief efforts. Dix began working with a new Western Commission that had been set up locally without consulting the national Sanitary Commission, and authorized the assignment of nurses to the region.

The Sanitary Commission was furious, urged the War Department to overrule Frémont's order, and renamed itself the U.S. Sanitary Commission. The Sanitary Commission's members blamed Dix for the new commission, although Eliot maintained that Frémont had acted only on Eliot's suggestion. The commission began to condemn Dix and belittle her as an incompetent, pathetic do-gooder, and it quickly became vengeful. One member, landscape architect Frederick Law Olmsted, published a nationwide notice that the Sanitary Commission was the only organization that could provide relief to the troops. When Dix objected that the announcement hurt her efforts to collect donations, Olmsted claimed he never knew about this part of her work. But the commission's meeting room was across the street from her house, where she stored donations, so Dix called Olmsted's response "strange."

As a final blow, the WCAR announced that it would not send any more nurses to Dix, claiming that her nurses had "a very uncertain semi-legal position, with poor wages and little sympathy," as Olmsted put it. These charges were true, but the WCAR's action left Dix to find and train nurses entirely by herself. This time, Dix could not prevail by hard work. She had always labored alone, in a world of personal relationships and individual discipline. But her skills were useless in a nation of bureaucracies and committees, and she began to fade away. By November 1861, she had shrunk from 139 to 99 pounds. Gaunt and wearing glasses, Dix had begun to look old.

In the summer of 1862, the Union suffered heavy losses while attempting to invade Virginia. After a week of bloody fighting, the Union was forced to retreat. More than 16,000 Union soldiers were wounded and killed, desperately straining the army's medical department. With few other resources, the government became keenly interested in recruiting women nurses.

Dr. Joseph K. Barnes took over as Acting Surgeon General in August 1863, and immediately began reorganizing nurses. As WCAR member Jane Woolsey later wrote, Barnes's plan "practically abolished the office of General Superintendent of Nurses." Dix could approve nurses but could not assign them to hospitals unless the surgeon in charge requested them. Nurses could avoid Dix altogether if they were "specially appointed by the Surgeon General."

A few weeks later, Barnes informed a young volunteer that he "both could and would appoint ladies at the request of a surgeon *irrespective* of *age, size, or looks*," and that the changes were made "to allow Surgeons to choose their *own* nurses, as many objected to Miss Dix's." Nurses stayed under Barnes's direct control for the rest of the war.

Unwilling to give up her position, Dix continued to approve the assignments issued by the medical department. Georgeanna Woolsey was amused when Dix confirmed her assignment to a military hospital near Philadelphia, writing she had "a good-natured laugh over a visit from Miss Dix, who, poor old lady, kept up the fiction of appointing all the army nurses." Thanks to both the WCAR's nurses and Dix's work, however, nursing came to be seen as a woman's paid profession, instead of a man's job, and thousands of women entered the field over the next decades.

Dix did find some other work inspecting prisoners of war. Negotiations about prisoners between the North and South had broken down, and both sides were housing captured soldiers in prisons. Dix informed Union General Benjamin F. Butler that she would like to help negotiate new prisoner exchanges. She was aghast at the condition of returning Union prisoners, whom she described as "mere skeletons gasping out a *murdered* life." After meeting with Butler, Dix began inspecting Union prisons.

Unfortunately, Dix and Butler worked at cross-purposes. He hoped that she would provide lurid descriptions of Union prisons that would convince the South to restart prisoner exchanges. Instead, the loyal Dix reported that the North ran model institutions. Butler sent her to Point Lookout, Maryland, the largest Union prison, expecting a litany of horrors; instead, Dix declared that "there was nothing which could be objected to, and so much to commend that I sum up all in saying that there is no [change] called for."

A month before Dix visited, prison officials in Elmira, New York, had predicted that all 8,000 prisoners would perish within a year if they continued to die at such a rapid rate. Incredibly, Dix reported that the Confederate soldiers

Despite the fact that Point Lookout military prison in Maryland was known for its horrific conditions, Dix declared after a visit that "there was nothing which could be objected to."

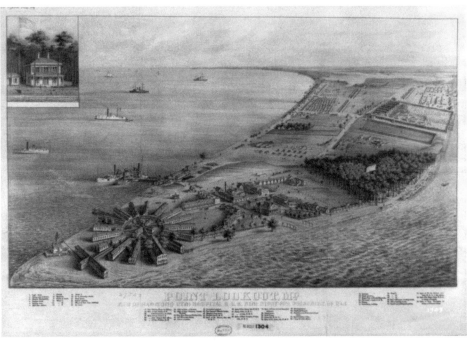

were getting adequate care, and that illness was rare. Dix's devotion to the Union cause made her blind to the Confederate prisoners' suffering. Butler was unable to arrange a new prisoner exchange, but Dix continued to interview Union prisoners about Southern prison conditions for the rest of the war.

Dix finally resigned as superintendent of women nurses in August 1865. She wrote to Anne Heath, "Thank heaven the War is over. I would that its memories also could pass away." Observers claim that Dix would say, "This is not the work I would have my life judged by!" over and over again. She avoided biographers and interviews and destroyed many of her papers. When Secretary of War Edwin Stanton told Dix that she ought to be publicly thanked by Congress for her efforts, Dix asked only to be given an American flag.

After the Civil War, Dix aged rapidly. In this 1838 photograph, she still wears her trademark plain white collar and simply coiled hair.

MORE TRAVEL, MORE BATTLES

Dix returned to Boston from Washington, D.C., in November 1865, and in her typical manner arrived on Anne Heath's doorstep with no advance notice. It was a woeful homecoming. Susan Heath noted in her diary that Dix was "terribly worn," as were the Heaths. Grace Heath, Anne Heath's niece, had suddenly collapsed and died in August 1864, three months after announcing her engagement. There was nothing Dix could do to help.

Instead, Dix went to New York to prevent another nontherapeutic mental hospital from being built. Twenty years earlier, Dix would have supported the bill, which called for building a hospital for patients who would not receive any treatment. At that time, she had pleaded for facilities for "the *incurable insane,* who, lost for life to the exercise of a sound understanding . . . are at once the most dependent and most unfortunate of human beings." Now, Dix believed that therapeutic asylums could cure almost all inmates, so that institutions for incurable cases were unnecessary. She recruited medical superintendents to testify that the state needed more therapeutic asylums, not custodial housing for incurable patients.

Many prominent New York doctors opposed Dix's campaign. A generation of physicians had seen that most patients in state mental hospitals either died there or left without being cured. John Chapin, superintendent at the Brigham Hall asylum in western New York, spoke for his generation when he wrote in 1867 that moral treatment was unscientific and that he would rather wait for "the revelations which the microscope will furnish." In the end, the New York legislature quickly approved funds for a new custodial institution and created a commission to find a site for a therapeutic mental hospital.

Dix began traveling again, helping mental hospital campaigns in Indiana, Pennsylvania, and Ohio. Despite this burst of activity, she was slowing down. She no longer had the same influence as before the Civil War, and her personal connections had been replaced by new state bureaucracies. By June of 1868, she wrote to Elizabeth Rathbone, "It is no longer needful to labor so incessantly for the insane," adding that "liberal acts by private individuals, with just Legislation in the States, keep pace with the necessities of a fast increasing population."

It was time for a vacation. In April 1869 she joined William Greenleaf Eliot's family for a journey to the Pacific coast, where Dix was awed by the natural beauty. California's Yosemite Valley, Washington's Mount Rainier, and dozens of other sights prompted her to claim that "scenes that profoundly impress the least observing and serious, move the very inner-most depth of the devout soul." Just as in her days at Oakland, she spent hours writing descriptions of flowers and insects; she measured the diameter of trees and contemplated just how the landscape was formed.

Dix spent the winter of 1869–70 traveling through the South, where postwar devastation and poverty kept many states from improving public mental hospitals. She told Anne Heath she would "put out of mind the terrible past . . . and take up the line of work here where I left it in 1860."

After arriving in Columbus, Ohio, in April 1870, Dix grew ill and was diagnosed with malarial fever. She traveled to the New Jersey State Lunatic Asylum, her favorite of all the hospitals she helped found, in an express railroad car.

Dix spent the next three years recovering from the disease at the New Jersey Asylum, her brother Joseph's home in Boston, and a friend's home in Washington, D.C. She did good works on a personal scale; she gave William Greenleaf Eliot's son Thomas $1,000, almost a third of her yearly income, to travel to New York to treat his blindness, and she helped place a fountain of pure drinking water near Boston's Custom House.

By December 1873, she was back to "*full* working ability," as she wrote to Anne Heath. Determined to defend her asylums, Dix traveled to Pennsylvania to help block the state from transferring convicts from prisons to state mental hospitals. This affront to moral therapy alarmed Dix, who stated that the mixing of patients and "murderers, burglars, horse thieves & c." would destroy the patients' self-respect. Ignoring Dix's objections, the legislature approved the plan to mix prisoners and patients in May 1874.

As always, Dix traveled in the face of failure, this time through the Midwest. Some young doctors laughed at her. Others, mindful of her personal relationships with superintendents, respectfully befriended her. Trustees universally celebrated Dix, the driving force behind their hospitals. One, John Harper, wrote, "The hospitals are your children," and in another letter, he said that the hospital trustees "notwithstanding our Protestant and iconoclastic ideas . . . regard you as its *patron saint*, and time will only hallow the association." Dix even allowed these admirers to hang portraits of her in the hospital halls—portraits that were painted from an antebellum picture of her looking young and hopeful.

While Dix rested in Boston that winter, a woman named Elizabeth Packard was storming Congress. She had been committed to the Illinois State Hospital for the Insane in 1860 solely on the basis of her husband's request, and she spent three years trapped there before a judge declared she was sane. Packard then began a state campaign to expand the rights of all people committed to mental hospitals without their consent—especially married women. She also worked with suffragist Elizabeth Cady Stanton to create legislation so that married women could control the money they earned, instead of giving it to their husbands. Packard herself earned money by selling books about her life as an inmate.

The Illinois state legislature unanimously passed Packard's "personal liberty bill" in 1867. She went on to lobby other states to limit involuntary commitment. In January 1875, she petitioned Congress to have the post office put secure mailboxes in all mental hospitals.

Packard disturbed Dix. Packard did not appear to be a "benevolent woman reformer" like Dix, who tried to fulfill traditional ideas of womanhood. Dix still believed that women were morally superior to men, and that the only public role for a woman was to be a pure-hearted reformer who labored selflessly on behalf of others. By contrast, Packard was interested in power, and worked to give women more power in their marriages and control over their own money. Despite all her work and her Civil War experiences, Dix still believed that women should be concerned with the home, not public affairs, and should be content as wives and mothers. Packard was a threat to Dix's ideals—and to Dix's friends, the hospital superintendents, who saw the mailboxes as a declaration that the patients could not trust their doctors and bitterly opposed them.

In Washington, Packard collected signatures supporting her mailbox bill and spoke to the House committee on postal affairs. Dix quietly wrote letters to her allies, coordinating efforts with her friend Charles Nichols, the superintendent of the Washington, D.C., Government Hospital for the Insane. Packard's bill failed; it was Dix's last political success.

The next few years were difficult for Dix. Her brother Joseph died in February 1878; Anne Heath followed him two months later. Dix had outlived much of her generation, and her own health was declining. The malaria returned, often making her legs too swollen and weak for her to walk.

In October 1881, Dix traveled to the New Jersey State Lunatic Asylum and collapsed. In early November, the hospital trustees voted to allow the superintendent to care for Dix at the hospital for as long as necessary. Dix never left the hospital. She had her estate's executors create a charitable trust fund to help young women learn to be wives and mothers and to help young men learn a trade. She asked William Greenleaf Eliot to lead a simple funeral service for her, but Dix did not tell him where she ought to be buried. As a citizen of the entire nation, she could not imagine one place where she could permanently reside.

But Dix was not ready to die yet. She became stable, if not well, and settled into her top-floor suite with her hundreds of letters, newspaper clippings, and photographs. Although she finally authorized her biography, she kept a packet in the top drawer of her desk marked "Family papers to be destroyed unopened." She turned away most visitors, and when her hand grew so shaky that she was no longer able to write letters, she refused to dictate them to a secretary. Still concerned with her self-discipline, Dix was embarrassed by the fact that her friends sent her Madeira wine to ease her pain—and that she drank it. She sometimes read aloud to the asylum inmates; John Ward, the asylum superintendent, thought she was the most expressive reader he had ever heard.

Dix was unable to leave her bed or sleep at night during the winter of 1881–82, and she was very much alone. Ward ordered staff to sit with her, but Dix threw women out if she thought they were improperly dressed. Dix begged William Greenleaf Eliot to come visit her again, but he wrote to his nephew, "What can be done? Nothing that

I can see. She will grow weaker & become more anxious to see us, but neither of us could be there long, at a time & to go back & forward takes more strength & money than either of us has to spare." When Eliot died in January 1887, Dix was shaken.

On July 18, 1887, Dix died in her sleep. She was buried in Mount Auburn Cemetery in Cambridge, Massachusetts. Laid near the graves of William Ellery Channing, Samuel Gridley Howe, and Charles Sumner in a wooded park built by Boston Unitarians to bless the dead with beauty, she was finally at rest.

Dix helped found the State Asylum for the Insane in Morristown, New Jersey, where she spent the last years of her life.

AFTERWORD

Dorothea Dix chose to work alone, but she was not the only woman activist in the United States—or even in her small Boston circle. The writer Lydia Maria Francis, who co-edited a children's magazine with Dix, went on to become Lydia Maria Child, editor of the *National Anti-Slavery Standard,* the weekly newspaper of the American AntiSlavery Society. Anne Heath's friend Elizabeth Palmer Peabody became a publisher and education activist, establishing the first kindergartens in the United States and holding philosophical conferences for women. During Dix's public life, Boston was crowded with women abolitionists, suffragists, education reformers, and philosophers—women who supported each other and worked together to change their society.

As Dorothea Dix retired from public life, women reformers such as Josephine Shaw Lowell called for the "scientific" prevention of poverty by systematically studying the poor. Jane Addams founded Hull House to aid the poor in Chicago two years after Dix died, and she won a Nobel Peace Prize for her work in 1931. Unlike Dix, these women built organizations and labored on government committees for years to realize their dreams.

Even though she worked alone, Dix convinced thousands of people to build hospitals to provide moral treatment to the poor. She persuaded the nation that the government had an obligation to help citizens who had no money and no one to care for them. Unfortunately, the asylums she helped establish cured few patients, and quickly ceased to be calm, caring communities.

In 1879 an American doctor named Pliny Earle published a paper proving what many doctors had suspected for decades: No form of treatment was curing mental illness. Hospital superintendents from the 1820s onward had reported cures based on the proportion of people leaving their institutions who were considered "sane," and they ignored the patients who lingered in their hospitals for years. Some patients were "cured" and readmitted up to 46 times, adding to the number of "recoveries." Statistics from Scottish mental hospitals showed that 75 percent of patients admitted in 1858 were still ill 12 years later or had died uncured. Simply putting people with mental illness away in an orderly hospital did not cure them. Dix's moral treatment just did not work. Over time, states short-changed their overcrowded mental hospitals, allowing them to become filthy and chaotic, the opposite of the moral treatment centers Dix had recommended. Running the state mental hospitals was a strenuous, ill-paying job, and a career with little status. Talented doctors stayed away from the profession, leaving many posts to incompetent and slothful candidates.

When Dix started her campaigns in 1841, there were 2,000 mentally ill patients in institutions in the United States; by 1860, there were roughly 8,000. By 1955, there were 559,000 patients living in mental hospitals, and 2 out of 3 patients with schizophrenia spent their lives there. Once the mental hospitals were built, local governments heartily supported the idea that the state should keep people with mental illness in one central institution, apart from their communities and families.

Starting in the 1950s, however, new drugs made it easier for people with schizophrenia, depression, and other mental illnesses to live outside institutions. The states released their patients, but those with chronic mental illness often had no place to go. Having given patients to the state 150 years ago, local governments were slow to fund programs to help such people live in their communities—and to provide the halfway houses, nurses, and social workers the patients needed to help control their illnesses and cope with life. Many people cannot go home because they have no family or no relatives willing to provide the kind of care they need; instead, they live on the street. Without access to care, they often grow sicker.

In 1999 there were 61,700 Americans with mental illness in state mental hospitals and 200,000 Americans with mental illness in jails and prisons. If Dorothea Dix were alive today, she would be at the White House, lobbying for the resources to keep people with mental illness out of prison and in treatment programs.

CHRONOLOGY

April 4, 1802
Dorothea Dix is born in Hampden, Maine

1812
Moves with her family to Vermont

1816
Arrives in Worcester, Massachusetts, to live with an aunt; starts her first school

1821
Moves to Boston to live with her grandmother at Orange Court

1824
Publishes *Conversations on Common Things*

1826
Agrees to teach Sunday school for William Ellery Channing

1830
Travels with the Channings to St. Croix

1831
Starts new school for girls in Orange Court

1836
Sails to England and stays with the Rathbones in Liverpool

1839
Moves into Sarah Gibbs's home in Boston

March 28, 1841
Teaches Sunday school class at Middlesex County House of Correction in East Cambridge; objects to lack of heat in the cell of a "mad" inmate

January 19, 1843
Publishes *Memorial to the Legislature of Massachusetts*; begins national work to build mental hospitals

1845
Publishes *Remarks on Prisons and Prison Discipline in the United States*

June 27, 1848
Dix's bill for land grants to support institutions for the mentally ill in every state is introduced into the U.S. Senate

May 3, 1854
President Franklin Pierce vetoes Dix's land grant bill

September 1854
Begins European reform work

April 22, 1861
Takes on job of organizing Union nurses during Civil War

1875
Battles Elizabeth Packard over congressional bill for secure asylum mailboxes

July 18, 1887
Dies in Trenton, New Jersey

FURTHER READING

BY DOROTHEA DIX

Dix, Dorothea. *On Behalf of the Insane Poor: Selected Reports.* New York: Arno Press & *The New York Times*, 1971.

Lightner, David L., ed. *Asylum, Prison, and Poorhouse: The Writings and Reform Work of Dorothea Dix in Illinois.* Carbondale: Southern Illinois Univ Press, 1999.

ABOUT DORTHEA DIX

Brown, Thomas J. *Dorothea Dix: New England Reformer.* Cambridge, Mass.: Harvard University Press, 1998.

Dannett, Sylvia. *Noble Women of the North.* New York: Thomas Yoseloff, 1959.

Gollaher, David. *Voice for the Mad: The Life of Dorothea Dix.* New York: Free Press, 1995.

Marshall, Helen. *Dorothea Dix, Forgotten Samaritan.* Chapel Hill: University of North Carolina Press, 1937.

Parrish, William E. "The Western Sanitary Commission," *Civil War History,* March 1990.

Schlaifer, Charles. *Heart's Work: Civil War Heroine and Champion of the Mentally Ill.* New York: Paragon House, 1991

Wilson, Dorothy Clarke. *Stranger and Traveler: The Story of Dorothea Dix, American Reformer.* Boston: Little Brown, 1975.

MENTAL HEALTH CARE

Brieger, Gert H. *Medical America in the Nineteenth Century.* Baltimore: Johns Hopkins University Press, 1972.

Grob, Gerald N. *Mental Institutions in America.* New York: Free Press, 1973.

Winerip, Michael. "Bedlam on the Streets," *New York Times Magazine,* May 22, 1999.

REFORMERS

Cott, Nancy F. *Bonds of Womanhood: "Women's Sphere" in New England 1780–1835,* 2nd ed. New Haven, Conn.: Yale University Press, 1997.

Davico, Rosalba, ed. *The Autobiography of Edward Jarvis (1803–1884).* London: Wellcome Institute for the History of Medicine, 1992.

Kenschaft, Lori. *Lydia Marie Child: The Quest for Racial Justice.* New York: Oxford University Press, 2002.

Roth, Randolph A. *The Democratic Dilemma: Religion, Reform and the Social Order in the Connecticut River Valley of Vermont, 1791–1850.* New York: Cambridge University Press, 1987.

19TH-CENTURY AMERICA

Hiner, N. Ray, and Joseph M. Hawes, eds. *Growing Up in America: Children in Historical Perspective.* Urbana: University of Illinois Press, 1985.

Howard, Brett. *Boston: A Social History.* New York: Hawthorn Books, 1976.

Kaestle, Carl F. *Pillars of the Republic: Common Schools and American Society, 1780–1860.* New York: Hill and Wang, 1983.

Kirker, Harold, and James Kirker. *Bulfinch's Boston, 1787–1817.* New York: Oxford University Press, 1964.

Stilgoe, John R. *The Common Landscape of America, 1580 to 1845.* New Haven, Conn.: Yale University Press, 1982.

INDEX

PICTURE CREDITS

TEXT CREDITS

Margaret Muckenhoupt holds an A.B. from Harvard University and a Sc.M. from Brown University. She was formerly a research assistant at MIT and is the author of the Oxford Portraits in Science biography *Sigmund Freud: Explorer of the Unconscious.*

Silver Creek High School
3434 Silver Creek Rd
San Jose, CA 95121